BANNER
OF THE
ANTICHRIST

Enzo Martucci

Edited by Kevin I. Slaughter
& MRDA

STAND ALONE

Banner of the Antichrist
by Enzo Martucci
Published by Union of Egoists and
Underworld Amusements
ISBN: 978-1-943687-36-7
STAND ALONE SA1295
First edition, April, 2025.

Originally published as *La Bandiera dell'Anticristo* in 1950.
English translation ©2024 Kevin I. Slaughter.
Editing by Kevin I. Slaughter & Daniel Acheampong.
Copyediting assistance by Alex Kies.
Design by Kevin I. Slaughter.

This is the first English-language translation of Enzo
Martucci's book. Explanatory footnotes without paren-
thetical appendix are by the author. Footnotes appended
with (L'Ed.) are by the original Italian editor. Footnotes
appended with (Ed.) are by the English translation editor.
Footnotes that cite sources may be from author or editor.

Quotations from Max Stirner's *The Ego and His Own* and
the Bible use the translations by Steven Byington.

This book is part of the *Stand Alone* series by the Union
of Egoists. *Stand Alone* is mixed format journal produced
at irregular intervals. The focus is egoism and the individuals associated with it.

More information:
www.UnionOfEgoists.com
www.UnderworldAmusements.com

PUBLISHER'S NOTE (2025)

As a publisher of radical, reactionary, Satanic, and intellectually and culturally dissident works—alongside other material of less objectionable nature—I have long resolved never to write a disclaimer for anything I publish, no matter how "difficult" or challenging the material may be. I will not refuse to publish works that interest me simply because some aspects do not align with my personal tastes, nor will I insist on publicly distancing myself from them. I trust my readers to engage thoughtfully with the content or to recognize that no disclaimer would serve their purpose.

For the sake of interest, context, and historical fidelity, I have translated and retained the original Italian publisher's disclaimer alongside Martucci's rebuttal. Even "Simonetti Walter," in his bombastic, black banner-waving introduction to a modern Italian edition, launches his preface with the question "Why reprint *La bandiera dell'anticrist* after sixty years? Why put back on the shelves a text that, in many aspects (personally), I do not agree with?" Walter emphasizes his distance from the text in a footnote, reprinting the reservations of its original publishers, who stated,

> "Of course, we do not share his individualistic theories, which—in our opinion—would not

push humanity towards anarchist freedom and equality but towards primitive barbarism, where only strength—not reason—dictated the norm of life."

Ironically, the idea that drew the sharpest critique from the original publishers is also the one most distinctly 'Stirnerian': the principle of *might is right*. It is precisely these radical and provocative ideas that I find essential to preserve, unfiltered and without apology, for readers capable of grappling with them. Indeed, Martucci pushes his ideas to such extremes that he might well serve as a cautionary tale.

KEVIN I. SLAUGHTER
BALTIMORE, MD
MARCH 2025

My freedom becomes complete only when it is my—*might*; but by this I cease to be a merely free man, and become an own man... You long for freedom? You fools! If you took *might*, freedom would come of itself. See, he who has *might* "stands above the law."
—Max Stirner, *The Ego and His Own*

4

PUBLISHER'S NOTE (1950)

Enzo Martucci? Just looking at him is enough to judge him: he has the face of a Lucifer escaped from Hell, and, consistent with his own theories, he lives in hatred of God and his enemies!

Of course, we do not share his individualistic theories, which—in our opinion—would not push humanity towards anarchist freedom and equality but towards primitive barbarism, where only strength—not reason—dictated the norm of life.

We also have many reservations about Martucci's moral conception, although we are amoral in the sense that morality is not codified, varying over time and space.

So the reader will ask, *Why did you publish this book which you disagree with?*

The reason is simple to explain: because we were told about Martucci — a philosophy professor — an anarchist from his youth who renounced the comforts his family had, an unyielding anti-fascist who was sent to prison and exile, forced into the harshest poverty because he was deprived of teaching, boycotted by his "comrades" and publishers, and therefore unable to express his thoughts through words and print; thus, we thought it right to extend him a fraternal hand.

That is why we have published this book, which we would have simply titled *Aberrations*, contributing to the spread of ideas we do not share but which should be known and discussed, as they lurk unknown in many restless souls, a secular legacy, increased by fascism and war.

Prepare, therefore, reader, your ear for unusual words, and do not be frightened by the many heresies contained in this book.

L.I.D.A.[1]

AUTHOR'S RESPONSE

I thank the publisher for the *demonic* presentation he has made of me and my book.

However, I remind him that all truly rebellious and innovative theories in the fields of philosophy and art, ethics and politics, have always been defined in all times and places as "aberrations."

Besides, what are these if not the flights of thought and the impulses of life, freed from every traditional and conventional form, from every Procrustean bed, from every forced frame?

ENZO MARTUCCI

---

1   Libreria Internazionale Di Avanguardia—the Italian publishers based in Bologna.

CONTENTS

The Catholic Octopus 9

Reply to a Theologian 40

Does Justice Exist? 56

Individualist Amoralism 67

The Holy Family 81

Nemo Me Impune Lacessit 100

Me and Mariani 120

No Prison, No Police 145

Italy is Dying 153

Light in the Darkness 168

THE CATHOLIC OCTOPUS

The kind Dr. Siccardi[2] defines me as "a gypsy, a wanderer, an unstable person who rebels against civilization." In a letter sent to a common friend, he adds that this unstable person

> ...wastes his strength and his talent, undeservedly remarkable, in the childish but monstrous attempt to excite spirits and drag them into anarchy, demonstrating the non-existence of the constant and uniform laws and order that ensure the development of universal life and allow the individual, humanity, and nature to achieve their goals and fulfill their destinies. He wants to overthrow reality into chaos, in which elements swirl confusingly. He wants to shatter society into individuals free from any ties and acting according to chance or need. And this is due to a personal impossibility to endure any discipline

---

2   Siccardi is a Catholic with a degree in philosophy, author of the book *Verità e sofismi* (*Truth and Sophisms*).

within and outside himself.

He takes refuge in relativism and attacks God, the absolute, every authority, and every rule to move according to his caprice and maximum fickleness in a disconnected and uncertain world. He prefers to aim his arrows against the Catholic Church because it maintains better than any other the unity of spirits and the concordance of efforts directed towards a goal of general elevation. He hates Catholicism, seeing in it the only true factor of cohesion, organicity, and progress. What has saved men from falling back into bestial violence for twenty centuries; what has prevented human intelligence from dying out in the darkness of the Middle Ages; what has preserved culture and civilization and now hinders the bloody explosion of war wanted by capitalism and Bolshevism?

This is what Dr. Roberto Siccardi says. And I feel sincerely moved by his words. Indeed, he is a good bourgeois, a man of order, a respectable person. He attends mass every Sunday, confesses and communicates at least once a year, was enrolled in the Fascist Party, and owns a *latifundium*[3] in Sicily. He has the conception of life learned in the priests' college where his adolescence passed. He worships family, hierarchy, rule, state, wise and providential authority. He loves, by temperament and conviction, the stabil-

---

3   A great landed estate with primitive agriculture and labor often in a state of partial servitude.

ENZO MARTUCCI

ity that unfolds in a composed, educated, moderate, circumscribed, directed way, that is, the stability that remains obedient to the discipline established by God and governments and the social classes that represent it on Earth. He is happy with his condition, which ensures him wealth in this world and Paradise in the other. He enjoys receiving bows from his porter and bowing himself in turn before the minister or general, the bishop, or the grand lady. He condemns, with all his soul, every revolt, every outbreak, every innovation that disturbs the normal course of things and the monotonous sequence of concatenated events. Therefore, his indignation towards a vagabond like me is fully justified, and I think that if I were a little less perverse, I should be ashamed in front of such a man and recite, like Papini, the Act of Contrition.

"All who appear to the commoner suspicious, hostile, and dangerous," writes Stirner, "might be comprised under the name "vagabonds"; every vagabondish way of living displeases him. For there are intellectual vagabonds too, to whom the hereditary dwelling-place of their fathers seems too cramped and oppressive for them to be willing to satisfy themselves with the limited space any more: instead of keeping within the limits of a temperate style of thinking, and taking as inviolable truth what furnishes comfort and tranquillity to thousands, they overleap all bounds of the traditional and run wild with their impudent criticism and untamed mania for doubt, these extravagating vagabonds. They form the class of the unstable, restless, changeable, *i.e.* of the prolétariat, and, if they give voice to their unsettled nature, are called 'unruly fellows.'"[4]

However, as "restless" and "unstable" as I may be, as deserving of the wrath and reproaches of the most kind-hearted Dr. Siccardi, I believe that, in the end, what I say and write is not all that crazy and monstrous. I doubt the questionable truth that the doctor accepts as a dogma, namely the existence "of order and laws, constant and uniform, that ensure the development of universal life and allow the individual, humanity, and nature to achieve their goals and fulfill their destinies."

Is there order in nature? Yes, but there is also disorder. Are there laws, constant and uniform, that ensure the development of universal life? Hume argued that nature may change in the future. Do individuals, humanity, and nature have their goals? Mechanists deny this. Can individuals, humanity, and nature fulfill their destinies? No one knows if they have a destiny or if they can achieve it if they do.

In *Philosophy of Revolution*,[5] Giuseppe Ferrari wrote,

> More circumspect and less wise, some limit themselves to announcing to us that the laws of the universe are constant, uniform, that the constancy and uniformity of the world laws are

---

4   Max Stirner, translated by Steven T. Byington, *The Ego and His Own*, New York: Benjamin R. Tucker 1907.

5   Giuseppe Ferrari, *Filosofia della rivoluzione* (*Philosophy of Revolution*), 1851.

ensured by space, time, substance, cause, being, which dominate objects and do not change. But the unity of being, the forces of substance, cause, space, and time are equally with order and disorder, progress and regression of the universe; they are conditions of what exists and they are nothing; they contain everything and do not impose on any being to remain what it is. The earth we inhabit does not arise from these generic entities, the globe is not the child of existence any more than the waters are the children of water. The government of the earth belongs to souls; they order the stones, the flowers, the animals; they dominate matter, from which they are not separated, because force never separates from the body. But even souls in their race through eternity, uniting with the progress and fate of war, are not yet nature, they are still blind and ignorant of the destiny that drives them, of the fate that awaits them. Don't think every being has to fulfill its destiny: around every tree, there are myriads of seeds and germs sacrificed to nourish it; around every animal, thousands and thousands of beings perish so that it may live; in nature, the being that fulfills its destiny enjoys a most fortunate privilege. What, then, is the point of so many declamations about the destiny of humanity when we ignore the data, the order, the purpose, in a word, the balance of the terrifying sacrifice that is constantly taking place in the vast ocean of creation? The very concept of destiny is distorted if we take it for our own benefit; destiny is fulfilled in two opposite senses, serving oneself, serving others, enjoying and suffering. Explain what the destiny of the lamb is, I will tell you what is yours, and perhaps you will see the progress of the land granted to a better race. Finally, what do uniformity and constancy of laws amount to in the midst of the metamorphosis of nature? To our ignorance; the more we enlighten ourselves, the more we realize that the stability of universal laws is shaken by the presence of altered elements, and we see that a modified substance can change the course of the universe. We accept uniformity and constancy as they reveal themselves, and let us not seek in the genera a fate that corroborates them, for there is no equation between the substance and the constancy of the universe: the two terms express only the necessity of the container and the content, and this same necessity could disappear with a new revelation. And if, to shake the current world, the proof of our instinctive conviction of natural faith, of the innate and expectation of seeing the present laws of matter perpetuated: let us pay attention to the faith, the security with which every summer insect lives, without suspecting the disaster that will destroy it in the evolution of winter. Let nature be left to nature.

Therefore, if we cannot prove that the process of

nature is governed by laws, constants, and uniformity that ensure the development of universal life in the same way, we can even less assert that the historical process of humanity is governed by laws that make it always progress on the same tracks towards a compulsory goal. Despite Dr. Siccardi's claims, reason cannot exclude the possibility of anarchy in both nature and society. And then, it all comes down to this: such anarchy is deplorable for Siccardi, desirable for me.

Just as nature could change in the future, with disorder taking over order because disorder, like order, has the unity of being and the forces of substance, cause, space, and time, society could also break down into unique individuals detached from all ties and acting according to chance or need.[6]

Such a perspective makes Dr. Siccardi cringe, as he loves regularity, constancy, the miracle of San Gennaro that happens every year, and the peasants who pay their rents on time. But I am attracted to such a mirage precisely because of my personal inability to endure any discipline within and without.

I see that every man is different from others, but they all desire freedom in which each can live in their own way, do as they please, and satisfy themselves as they like. Organized society forces all these different men to live in an identical way, to follow a single system, to accept a single morality, to obey the same law. Through the conformity it imposes, society seeks to

---

6   Also in my book *Beyond,* I argued that appearances can change, the nature we perceive may change in the future, and organized society may dissolve into anomie.

stifle in the individual everything that is particular, personal, and unique. It seeks to annihilate in man the instinctive need for freedom, replacing it with the slavish habit of obedience to superiors and gregarious existence. Therefore, organized society is the cause of the pain, slavery, and degeneration of most individuals.

That this state of affairs should remain eternal is the desire of the rulers, leaders, bosses, and all those who, in the name of the order they maintain, subject others to their authority and exploit them continuously. But it is not my desire because I love freedom, and I like to see around me people who also want to be free.

That's why I aspire to Anarchy, with a capital a, to the destruction of all the chains, moral and material, that bind individuals. When these individuals are free, they can understand each other in many different ways, and they may also fight when they cannot agree. But each will fight for themselves, for their own interest or feeling, and no longer for a cause imposed by leaders.

Siccardi says that I take refuge in relativism and attack God, the absolute, every authority, and every rule to move according to my caprice, and with the greatest fickleness, in a disconnected and uncertain world.

Certainly, I am a relativist because everything I know, everything I feel and think, is limited and contingent. I can never find the absolute, just like other humans, even those who claim to have discovered it

ENZO MARTUCCI

and who, in its name, burden humanity with chains. And it is precisely against these chains that I rebel because I want to be free to move as I please in a world that is free and changeable like me. And it will certainly be preferable to the old world, massive and square, that rests on the foundation of theology.

Siccardi asserts that, precisely, I prefer my attacks against the Catholic Church. However, while it is true that I have attacked this church with my writings and with numerous conferences held in many Italian cities, it is also true that I have not spared criticism of other churches and those schools and theories that, while professing to be agnostic or atheist, seek to replace an old dogma with a new one and want to put another authority in place of the Christian god.

For me, it is necessary to destroy the belief in every higher entity, in every principle that towers over the individual and that arouses in them the reverential fear, the feeling of inferiority, and the duty of submission. These metaphysical entities do not have an objective reality, a separate existence, but are products of human thought, which has become a slave to its own creations.

Some men have thought that there is an exalted God or the Homeland or the Conscience or Humanity, which, as a single and indivisible principle, is above human individuals. After having thought this thought, they communicated it to others for the purpose of earthly domination or collective enlightenment, and they succeeded in convincing or suggesting these others. Thus, everyone believed, everyone bowed down, and the reign of phantoms began in the world.

But it is from such servitude that the self must free itself. If he manages to understand that he himself is the only reality, thinking and acting, and that there is nothing above him, then he will truly become free. He may still encounter obstacles in the resistance that other men and nature will oppose him, but he will not see anything sacred in these obstacles that he will have to respect, and he will try to overcome them with his strength. Other men are my equals, and I am part of nature too, so why should I let myself be stopped by the barriers with which they try to stop my path? To their strength, I respond with mine, and if this is not enough to secure my victory, I can always try to increase it by any means. If, in the end, I find that I cannot succeed, I must attribute the blame to myself, to my lack of power; I know that my freedom ends where my strength ends, and if I do not manage to conquer a certain freedom, it is because my power has not granted it to me, but at least I have the satisfaction of having tried, of not having resigned myself to the renunciation that has been imposed on me.[7]

Instead, if I worship a phantom, I am forced to give up all the freedoms that it denies me, even if I have the strength to conquer them. I must remain

---

[7]   For me — though I am an individualist — this theory of force is not anarchy, as anarchy is harmonious coexistence, it is the civil life of a collective and not of savages who use their brute force to impose themselves and oppress others. (L'Ed.)

a slave forever; I cannot exercise my power or assert myself, but I am obliged to be content with what the master, in his magnanimity, grants me. That is why I think, with Stirner, that "it is with crime that the egoist[8] has always affirmed himself and has sacrilegiously overturned the holy idols from their pedestal. Breaking with the sacred or, better still, breaking the sacred can become general. It is not a new revolution that is approaching, but powerful, proud, without respect, without shame, without conscience, a crime grumbles with thunder on the horizon, and do you not see that the sky, pregnant with foreboding, darkens and falls silent?"

Siccardi, however, says that I fight the Catholic Church so much "because it maintains the unity of minds and the concordance of efforts directed towards a goal of general elevation better than any other."

But by what means does the church maintain this unity and concordance? With the principle of authority.

Christianity has always taught men to love, worship, and fear the Lord. God is the supreme craftsman, the creator of the Earth, man, and everything. He punishes us if we do not obey the law he has dictated; he rewards us if we instead observe that law. Therefore, to avoid divine wrath, we must think and act as God wants. We are required to renounce all earthly joys, to stifle the cravings of the flesh, the

---

8   Egoism can be bourgeois or anarchic; it all depends on how one defines egoism. (L'Ed.)

impulse of instincts, the drive of nature, because our soul must not give in to the allurements of the body that drag us into sin and distract us from the true life, which is that of the spirit. We must not only conform to God's will with our actions but also with our thoughts; if I think of committing a sin, take pleasure in this thought, and do not banish it with horror, I am equally guilty even if I do not commit the act prohibited by divinity. We men must also love each other fraternally, forgive each other for offenses, bear pain and adversity with resignation. We must be humble, docile, submissive, always ready to obey not only divine authority but also human authorities that God has established in this world.

> Let every soul be submissive to superior authorities; for there is no authority except by God, and those that there are are given their positions by God, so that he who sets himself against authority is opposing God's institution...[9]

Only in the event that earthly authority conflicts with divine authority and requires us to perform acts forbidden by God must we resist it. But we must resist passively, without violent rebellion, not obey but allow ourselves to be arrested, tortured, killed without defending ourselves with force. In every other case, we are compelled by God himself not only to serve but also to love and honor our masters.

---

9   Romans 13:1–2

Let as many as are under a yoke in servitude regard their masters as entitled to all honor, in order that God's name and the teaching may not be vilified. And let those who have believing masters not be disrespectful to them because they are brothers, but be the more their servants because those who enjoy the benefit are believers and loved ones.[10]

And again,

Domestics, be submissive to your masters in all fear, not only to the kind and reasonable but also to the cranky; for it is a credit if one bears troubles for the consciousness of God, when one suffers unjustly.[11]

As it is therefore clear, renunciation, resignation, love, obedience, that is, all Christian virtues, are imposed by God on men who accept them to avoid the wrath of the Heavenly Father, to escape Hell, and instead, become deserving of Paradise, where joys will be eternal. Therefore, according to Christianity, the unity of minds and the concordance of efforts are determined by the despotic will of a master who manages to be obeyed by servants, exploiting their cowardice, their fear of punishment, and their greed, that is, their thirst for reward and endless enjoyment.

The Christian makes a calculation: *I sacrifice*

---

10   1 Timothy 6:1–2
11   1 Peter 2:18–19

myself in this transitory life to gain happiness in the immortal afterlife. He is as selfish as the brigand who steals and kills to procure the pleasures of the Earth. Both calculate; both choose the means that seem best to them. The goal is the same: personal joy, which they seek to achieve through different paths. All those who have calculated in the same way and have embarked on the same path agree. Well, what is sublime in this? The unity of minds and the concordance of efforts are also found in a gang of outlaws who attack established society and must defend themselves against everyone alone.

But Christians, says Siccardi, aim at a goal of general elevation. What is this goal? For the early Christians, it was the conquest of Paradise, which they sought to reach by allowing themselves to be torn apart by beasts in the circus or by retreating into the desert to flagellate and fast or by castrating themselves, like Origen, to avoid carnal sin. The Christianity of the early centuries was delirious fanaticism that tended toward the physical annihilation of humanity through the pursuit of pain, the practice of chastity, and the maceration of the body. But after the Council of Nicea, having obtained the protection of the state, becoming the official religion, the Christian church transformed into a priestly caste that sought to secure, by all means, the dominion of this world.

The priests continued to preach to the faithful about renouncing earthly possessions, poverty, and humility, but for themselves, they wanted riches and

ENZO MARTUCCI

imposed on believers to strip themselves in favor of the church that identified with the clergy. They continued to teach evangelical love but at the same time added that those who did not believe in the pope and did not submit to his power were not brothers in Christ but wicked heretics who deserved to be exterminated with iron and fire. They always said that earthly authorities were ordained by God because these authorities honored and supported the ecclesiastical organization, granted lands and servants, and defended it from its enemies. But when some king or emperor was not loyal, the pontiff excommunicated him, released the subjects from the duty of obedience, and incited them, in the name of divinity, to overthrow the sovereign who had not wanted to serve the interests of the faith. Thus, Gregory VII invited not only the subjects but also the son and wife of the rebellious Caesar to revolt against Henry IV.

Hypocrisy replaced fanaticism; the duty to serve God and evangelical norms were changed to the obligation to blindly submit to the authority of the pope and the exploitation of the church. Ascetic morality became less rigid: the clergy practiced the sale of indulgences and absolved those sinners who paid money and promised their supine obedience to the orders of the ecclesiastics. The ideal that renounced the Earth, aspiring to Heaven, transformed into the ideal that aimed at the dominion of the Earth in the name of Heaven. The popes became autocrats, ferocious and intolerant, who interfered in political and social issues and claimed to command kings and peoples, shear flocks, and dispose of the world as they pleased. And "the goal of elevation" that, during primitive Christianity, humanity identified with the conquest of Paradise conditioned by the practice, in current life, of renunciation, chastity, resignation, and non-violence changed, under historical Christianity—that is, under Catholicism—into the conquest of Paradise through immediate submission to the priests, participation in the massacre of heretics, payment of money to the church, and belief in all the lies that the pope and his priests peddled.

Therefore, both before and after, what Siccardi calls the general goal of elevation was for men nothing more than a naive, selfish aspiration to a celestial place of joy that could only be achieved by serving a master: either God and the morality dictated by him, or the church that could also release from the obligations imposed by evangelical morality when it was useful for its earthly domination.

The retired Dr. Siccardi declares, with the ridiculous presumption of someone who does not know history, that "Catholicism, the only true factor of cohesion, organicity, and progress, is what has saved men for twenty centuries from falling back into bestial violence."

Well done, Doctor! You deserve, like Father Lombardi, the warm applause of all the devout women and sacristans in Italy.

However, if Voltaire could come out of the grave, he would give you a mocking slap.

And, please, tell me, have you forgotten the

massacre of the Arians ordered by the Eastern emperor Justinian at the instigation of the pope, who, for such incitement to murder, was put in jail by Theodoric? Have you forgotten the crusade against the Albigensians preached by Pope Innocent III and St. Dominic Guzman? One hundred thousand men, women, and children were mercilessly slaughtered by the fanatical hordes of Simon de Montfort. Is this how our species was saved from falling back into bestial violence?

And what do you think of the wars against the Turks, Doctor?

What do you say about the massacre that the soldiers of Godfrey of Bouillon carried out in Jerusalem?

And was it for Christian charity that the popes had the Waldensians and the Hussites massacred?

And was it out of love for their neighbor that the inquisitors burned alive millions of men for four centuries? And have you ever heard of the Te Deum of thanksgiving sung by Gregory XIII in St. Peter's when he learned that the Huguenots had been exterminated in Paris?

Come on, Doctor... History is not your strong suit.

Let's see if he is more skilled in logic. And, therefore, I propose the same question to you that I proposed to Professor Scremin in the debate I had with him in Montecatini Terme.

When the popes incited Catholics to war against heretics or Muslims, for the salvation of the faith or the liberation of Christ's tomb, they always said that they were inspired by the Holy Spirit. It is true that the Crusaders attacked with the cry of "God wills it."

Now there are two hypotheses: either the popes were lying, they were impostors, and it is not true that the Holy Spirit spoke and speaks through the mouth of a pope, or the pontiffs were telling the truth, and, in this case, it was the Holy Spirit who incited the slaughter of infidels. But the Holy Spirit is a person of the Divine Trinity. Another person of the same trinity, Christ, told men that they should not kill each other.

So what now? Is there a contradiction in God? Is there opposition between the persons who compose it, who are stopped with the same substance and have the same will and the same thought? One part of God tells us that we should never kill other men but love everyone and forgive our enemies. Another part of God imposes us to arm ourselves and slaughter the men who follow Muhammad, Mani, or Calvin.

And who should we believe? To whom are we obliged to obey?

Like Stirner, like Nietzsche, like Ibsen, I want the individual to be free and strong. I think that if I consider my freedom a right, that is, a faculty that others recognize in me, a concession that society grants me and ensures its respect to me, then I am not preparing to defend my freedom, and if society wants to withdraw the benefit granted to me, it can do so with impunity. Instead, if I value my freedom as my property, as Stirner says, that is, something that I conquer and preserve through my personal power, I try to develop my physical, intellectual, and volitional strengths to the fullest and find myself ready at all times to resist those who seek to overpower me.

All individuals must strive to become strong. Even though absolute equality among individual strengths is not and will never be possible, it will be possible to eliminate the excessive disproportion between one power and another. And I can defend myself even against those who prove stronger than me by opposing them with the means that I consider, from time to time, most appropriate. I will either react to the superiority of their muscles with the resources suggested by intelligence and cunning, or I will establish a free and revocable alliance with other individuals willing to help me, or I will find a different way to resist them. In short, when everyone is strong, an equilibrium will spontaneously arise among them and will often lead to an agreement even in cases where this agreement could not be reached by other means (reciprocal sympathy, need for cooperation, etc.).[12] Conversely, if some individuals resign themselves to remaining weak and defenseless, their neighbors will take advantage of them and reduce them to servitude.[13]

---

12   Not everyone will ever be equally strong enough to form a social balance of justice and freedom. (L'Ed.)
13   This is the history of nations that increasingly arm themselves to defend against aggressors: it is a history that ends in the balance of war. (L'Ed.)

The feeling of personal power as the only means of affirmation in the struggle for life is possessed by man in the state of nature and in some civilizations, such as the Greco-Roman one, which exalted natural energy while considering it a weapon that the individual should not use so much for his own benefit as for the interests of the family and the state. However, in Athens after Pericles and in Rome after Augustus, the traditional authorities weakened, social ties loosened, individualism prevailed, and everyone used their own strength for themselves.[14] When Christianity arrived, it condemned earthly life and the power that is useful for affirming ourselves in it and saw, in general, weakness, resignation, and renunciation the necessary conditions for earning our reward in the afterlife. As Christianity transformed into the Catholic Church, it wanted to keep man enslaved and abulic, to stifle in his soul every independence and every energy in order to more easily command and direct him in thought, feeling, and practical activity. That is why Christianity was, from the beginning, the most bitter enemy of pagan civilization and contributed effectively to its destruction, along with the barbarian invasions and the upheavals that they caused.

Therefore, Siccardi demonstrates a pyramidal ignorance when he asserts that "Christianity prevented human intelligence from extinguishing in the darkness of the Middle Ages and preserved civilization

---

14   Precisely what was intended to be... demonstrated! (L'Ed.)

and culture."

But how? If pagan literature and art were an apotheosis of earthly life and the passions that make it shine, if classical philosophy and science represented a continuous search that was never satisfied with the results achieved, ultramundane and dogmatic Christianity had to necessarily fight against them. And so, it did.

Tertullian firmly asserted that a Christian could not teach ancient wisdom, and Saint Jerome imagined in a vision that, called to the final judgment, he would be reproached for the fault of being a follower of Cicero while professing to be a Christian. In his letter to Leta on the education of his daughter Paula and in another epistle to his friend Gaudenzio on the education of his daughter Pacatula, Saint Jerome advised that young girls should eat in such a way as to always be hungry and not listen to musical instruments in order not to become victims of imagination and sensitivity. And with such teachings, the pedagogical concept of asceticism, which aims at the annihilation of the individual and his physical and psychic needs, found its complete manifestation in the womb of the church,

The monks of Saint Cyril incited the Alexandrian plebs to the massacre of Hypatia and the Neoplatonic philosophers, and the priests urged the edict by which Justinian, in 529, closed the school of Athens and put an end to Greek philosophy.

Pope Leo I ordered the Palatine Library to be set on fire, and the clergy favored the resurgence of ignorance resulting from the destruction of classical civilization and the barbaric invasions and dominations. And when, towards the seventh century, faced with the resurgent need for culture, the church had to adapt to the times and open parish and abbey schools, it only taught religious instruction. So much so that in 789, Charlemagne obliged priests to instruct all children, both noble and common, and to teach them not only catechism and psalms but also grammar, arithmetic, singing, and music. And to give strength to this provision, he chose the learned Alcuin of York as his collaborator.

In convents where zealous monks preserved and transcribed ancient works that had survived destruction, this effort was determined more by the need to interpolate the works to make them useful for the purposes of the church than by the intention to benefit culture. Thus, among the many crude interpolations, there was the one with which Giuseppe Flavio made known, in his *Ancient History of the Jews*: the historical existence of Jesus and his quality as Messiah. But if Flavio had really written that, he would no longer have been Jewish but Christian. Instead, until the third century, the church saw the Israeli historian as a misconceiver of Christ. Origen said of Flavio that "although he does not believe in Jesus as Messiah, he sometimes comes close to the truth." This shows that the interpolation was made after the third century and, probably, precisely in the era of the erudite monks who falsified texts.

After the Middle Ages, which marked the

absolute dominance of dogma over consciences, priests did not give up in the face of the Renaissance but sought to fight it with its own weapons. And well-educated and cunning priests used the school to keep men ignorant and discipline to stifle personality.

The Jesuits sought to destroy the originality and independence of the self in every student, who, transformed into an automaton, had to feel and think, want and act, as the masters suggested. Ignatius of Loyola wrote in his *Spiritual Exercises*, "To avoid error, we must hold as a principle that what I see as white, I believe to be black if the hierarchical church establishes it as such." And the followers of the Spanish saint applied the teachings of the founder of their order, demanding blind obedience from the student, whose actions were monitored not only by superiors but also by means of spying and denunciation by fellow students. Even in their feelings, they sought to investigate, and he who had a natural, innocent impulse of freedom was condemned and punished, while casuistry absolved the other, guilty one if he had acted with the intention of benefiting the church.

The Jesuits left the common people in ignorance and the other classes in that half-education that is worse than ignorance. Their pupils knew a little about everything, but only what was explained by their teachers and judged by them. They were, in a word, miserable slaves, devoid of critical thinking and independence of thought, incapable of personal initiative, and destined to be always directed by the will of the confessor.

In this way, Catholicism saved culture. And so, those shrewd intellectuals, like Dr. Siccardi, who are striving so hard to give the school back to the priests and prepare a future generation of ignoramuses and sycophants are trying to strengthen it even more.

Finally, the seraphic Dr. Siccardi drops the last bomb. "The church," he declares, "is now hindering the war that is wanted by capitalism and Bolshevism."

Shameless lie! The Vatican, allied with Anglo-Saxon capitalism, is preparing for war against Russian Bolshevism.

If the Papacy wanted to fight the danger of the much-discussed conflict between East and West, it should call for a crusade for peace. It should urge its priests, in all countries belonging to the Stalin or Truman blocs, to preach against war, to convince Christians not to slaughter each other and not to present themselves for military service when called upon. This would be truly evangelical, and even if the priests were exposed to persecution for having advised passive resistance, they should face adversity with a joyful spirit and persevere in their action.

The pontiff could prohibit Catholic workers from working in factories engaged in war production. He could use the numerous and powerful organizations that depend on the church to agitate public opinion and turn it against war. He could spend at least part of the immense wealth he possesses to fuel the pacifist propaganda and subsidize those who would be affected by the sabotage of the war effort.

ENZO MARTUCCI

It would also be the duty of the Holy Father to intervene between enemy governments, perform acts of reconciliation, and use his spiritual authority and moral influence on the people to pressure the leaders of rival states and induce them to reach an agreement. The pope should do this, and even if his efforts were unable to prevent a future massacre, they would always remain as evidence of consistency with the spirit of the gospel that he claims to represent.

But the pontiff does none of this. Instead, he supports the policy of the American government and urges the clerical or bourgeois governments of Western European nations to align with the bloc that will provide cannon fodder to Truman in the war against Russia. In all countries of the world, priests, instructed by the Vatican, do not preach peace but attack Bolshevism, instill hatred against the Bolsheviks in people's hearts, and prepare the souls of the faithful for the holy crusade that, with atomic bombs, will bring down Stalin's tyranny. In Catholic countries that adhere to the Eastern bloc, such as Poland and Hungary, the clergy exploits the trust that a good part of the people have in it and incites believers against the government, secretly prepares the insurrection, and obstructs with all possible means the work of communist leaders. In Hungary, Cardinal Mindszenty was sentenced because he was accused of conspiring to restore the Habsburgs.

In Western countries, on the other hand, priests strongly support anti-communist governments, endorse the strengthening of armies and war preparation, and urge citizens to remain disciplined in obeying all orders of their leaders and all measures that they adopt for the public good.

In Germany, France, and Italy, Vatican agents recruit the relics of Nazism and fascism—followers of Pétain, Ustasha exiles, war criminals—and organize them, subsidize them, and form special units that will serve to slaughter our Bolsheviks and strike the first blows against the Russians at the opportune moment.

The pope actively works to obtain the reconstruction of German unity from the Anglo-Americans. In exchange, however, the Germans will create an army to fight Bolshevism. And when Stalin is overwhelmed, and the Eastern Bloc is defeated, the Catholic government that the pope will have appointed in Berlin and that will have been the soul of the war against Russia will remain definitive precisely because it will be surrounded by the light of victory. The unrepentant German nationalists will support the government that will have restored independence to the homeland and revenge against the Bolsheviks. And the Vatican will dominate the German people through its leaders, who will receive orders from Rome.

Similarly, Italy, France, and Belgium will remain under clerical-fascist governments that have directed the Latin people in their attack against the Slavs. These governments, initially installed with the help of the Anglo-Americans, who saw them as the most suitable instruments for leading the Westerners

ENZO MARTUCCI

to slaughter, will later depend only on the pope. Other Catholic governments will be established in Hungary, Poland, Czechoslovakia, and Romania because in these countries, too, Catholics inspired by the Vatican will have led the fifth columns against the communists. Franco will remain immovable in Spain and Salazar in Portugal. Thus, the pope will command Europe, and through the clerical governments loyal to him, he will be able to impose blind obedience to the church on the peoples. Pius XII will realize the theocratic dream of Gregory VII and Innocent III. And the Anglo-Saxons will willingly adapt to this state of affairs, which will guarantee them the maintenance of order from the Atlantic to the Urals.

With this happy illusion, the Vatican not only does not hinder the war but desires and prepares for it as much as possible. It fights Bolshevism not because Stalin is a dictator and Russia a barracks in which the proletarians march under the whip of the comrade-corporal; the Vatican does not care about this at all, and as it has always agreed with all tyrants, it would also agree with Stalin if Stalin accepted to share power with the pope. But the ambitious Asian wants to rule alone, and Pius XII aligns himself with the Anglo-Saxon capitalism that contends with Bolshevism for the lordship of the Earth. The bankers of London and New York will allow the pontiff to govern the European peoples because the pontiff will allow them to economically exploit these peoples. Then, even if the pope goes a little further and restores the stakes, Master Titta, and mandatory confession, the Puritans of England and the Masons of America will not be scandalized by so little but will let it go, calculating the enormous advantage that will come to them from the entanglement of the masses in the Catholic fold, where every economic demand of the proletarians and every revolt against the yoke of capital will be suffocated with the teaching of resignation, the promise of Paradise and Torquemada's methods applied to the rioters.

From Europe, Catholicism will conquer the rest of the world. With the help of the Vatican, Peron will dominate the entire South America. In the United States, Catholics will become increasingly stronger. Japan, where papist agents work actively, will finally convert to the Christian faith. Capitalism and Catholicism, tenaciously allied, will tyrannize humanity, unified under their lash.

On the other hand, Stalin also aspires to conquer the globe and reunite humankind in the shackles of Bolshevism.

And so, to serve the interests and ambitions of the Kremlin clique or the rival plutocratic-clerical clique, the sheep-like people will allow themselves to be dragged to the slaughter and will exterminate each other with atomic bombs and cosmic rays, with bacteriological means and toxic gases. Our species will perish in the bloody vortex of the last world war. The scientific years will destroy it. And it will die because men, instead of remaining free and unbound as nature had created them, have wanted to organize themselves, bind themselves, and depend on the leaders who, profiting from the general subjection, dispose, at their pleasure, of the freedom and life of all.

Siccardi says that anarchy would annihilate humanity. Instead, it will be precisely the herd instinct that will push it into the grave.

However, this could be avoided.

I do not believe that history is governed by fixed laws that inexorably propel it towards a final goal: human unity in the cosmopolitan state or the disappearance of our kind through the violent conflicts provoked by the rivalry of nations.

History proceeds by chance. Its path is not straight but zigzag. It does not constantly advance towards a single goal but continuously changes its purposes. And this happens because it is not determined by a single factor (Hegel's ideal factor or Marx's economic factor) but by a plurality of contrasting factors, ideal, sentimental, economic, sexual, and even by the imponderable, that is, by the mysterious forces that emanate from the obscure recesses of our nature and sometimes compel us to perform certain actions without us being able to explain the reason.

Therefore, historical facts are often incomprehensible. We see situations that suggest a certain result, produced by the already-existing conditions. Instead, the result is often the opposite of what was expected.

In Italy, in 1920, everyone was expecting the socialist revolution. There were the conditions that should have brought it about. Instead, we had the fascist counter-revolution.

In 1940, everyone believed in Germany's victory. The Germans had conquered Europe, England was isolated, and America was powerless to help because it would take at least three years to adapt its industry to war production and prepare for intervention. Hitler had secured his back with the commercial and friendship treaty signed with Russia. He could direct all his forces against the English, take advantage of the superiority of his air fleet to pulverize the enemy defenses, destroy the major cities of the island, and terrorize and depress the opposing people. Then, at the right moment, he would land his soldiers and occupy Great Britain. King George's government would have to beg for peace, and Nazism would emerge victorious from the war. Even if, for any reason, the landing in England failed, Hitler could have passed with his armies through Spain, which would not have opposed him. After conquering Gibraltar, occupying northern Africa and Egypt, he would have gone on to the Indies. Turkey, Persia, and the Arab countries would not have dared to resist him but would have joined him. The German motorized forces would have reached the Ganges, and the English, struck at the heart of their empire, would have had to surrender.

Instead, Hitler attacked Russia, which at that time did not bother him and with which, if ever, he could have settled accounts after his victory over England. He consumed his power in the last blood

ENZO MARTUCCI

duel with the Moscow giant, gave America time to arm itself, and the English time to strengthen themselves, and, finally, was defeated.

Even now, in the world, the third annihilating war appears inevitable.

Stalin wants to conquer the globe, but the Anglo-American capitalism that currently dominates it is not willing to let him. Ideologies once again serve as a mask for the most unbridled interests, and under the pretext of defending Christian civilization or Marxism-Leninism, the ambition and greed of the two opposing cliques that aspire to exploit and oppress all humanity are hidden.

Only the people could prevent the terrible clash by rebelling, but it is likely that they will not do so and will allow themselves to be dragged into the massacre because they are gregarious, servile, used to obeying, and drinking all the nonsense that the rulers peddle.

And the billowing black banner would be the symbol of catharsis that would transform the sheep destined for slaughter into a free and strong man, who would know how to live for himself, for his freedom, and for the different goals he would set for his actions.

REPLY TO A THEOLOGIAN

Some time ago, I had a debate in Terni with the theologian Zòffoli that was abruptly interrupted by the intervention of the authorities, preventing me from responding to the friar's answer. That's why I'm doing it now on these pages. And I begin by establishing the difference that separates philosophy from theology.

I declared, "Philosophy is the science that seeks to reduce the plurality of phenomena to an intelligible unity. Instead, theology attempts to reduce this plurality of phenomena to a unity that is neither perceptible nor intelligible. Therefore, theology, while deriving from philosophy, is sharply opposed to it."

To my statement, Zòffoli countered, "I say that throughout the centuries, philosophy has always asserted itself as the search for the infinite, which, for this reason, is intelligible. The history of thought is the search for the undefinable absolute that cannot be reduced to human concepts."

I agree, Professor Zòffoli! But I was about to

explain to you then, and I explain it to you now, why, on that evening, the Marxist mayor prevented me from doing so. While philosophy endlessly seeks, without ever finding, this intelligible absolute, theology, on the contrary, believes it has found, known, and understood it and wants to explain its existence to everyone with the three famous proofs that I subsequently criticized: God proven by ideas, by causes, and by purpose.

Regarding the objections I raised against the first proof, Zòffoli was quick to declare, "It is not true that Anselm of Canterbury's argument, as Martucci said, is the greatest argument for proving the existence of God. Secondly, what my opponent spoke of was not the ontological argument but rather the fourth way."

Descartes and Leibniz did not agree with Zòffoli, considering that the proof by ideas was the greatest compared to the others. But that doesn't matter. Let's see, instead, what the ontological argument proves and whether its demonstration can withstand criticism.

"Our thought," said Anselmo, "can think of that which nothing greater can be thought." But this cannot exist in the intellect alone because if it did, one could think of something greater, namely that which exists in reality, which contradicts the assumption. Therefore, there exists without doubt something than which nothing greater can be thought, both in the intellect and in reality."

But let us see if this is true. I think of an island than which no greater can be thought. An immense, bizarre, extraordinary island, crossed by rivers vaster than oceans and teeming with mountains that rise up to the stars. I search for this island in reality, and I do not find it. I traverse the world, far and wide, to track it down, but I do not find it. Therefore, the island does not exist. It exists in my thought but not in reality. Therefore, what is found in thought does not necessarily have to be found in reality.

Now let us consider Anselmo's other argument, the fourth way, which Zòffoli accused me of confusing with the ontological argument.

"I," says the saint of Aosta, "in the presence of any object, conceive a superior object in power, in size, in beauty. I can always surpass every finite perfection; surpassing the finite, I can conceive a being whose perfection is infinite. But the being that is supposed to be perfect must combine all perfections; existence is a perfection, and I must add the perfection of existence to the being that I conceive to be supremely perfect. Therefore, the perfect being exists."

To Anselmo's demonstration, I objected in my conference that it is impossible to conceive of a being in which all perfections are united because they are contradictory. The perfection of man, which is strength, virility, energy, would be the imperfection of woman: it would make her a virago. The perfection of woman, which is sweetness, kindness, refinement, would deform man: it would transform him into an effeminate. Can one conceive, therefore, a being that in itself would unite all perfections? That would be both perfectly great and perfectly small, perfectly good and perfectly bad, perfectly beautiful and perfectly ugly? This being would be a monster, so strange and grotesque that human thought could not conceive of it.

Zòffoli quickly countered with a tale to demonstrate that "all perfections are reduced to the same simplicity in which all perfections reconcile with the classical concept of the absolute. Perfections are not contradictory; they do not exclude each other, but they complete each other because they are perfections of beings, different in form but equal in substance."

Well said, Professor Zòffoli! In the absolute, opposites unify, genders disappear, diversities vanish, everything reduces to unity, to the same substance, to one being. But perfections are perfections of genders, that is, of those manifestations of the absolute that have assumed particular forms, different from those taken by other manifestations. Now, if manifestations disappear by returning to the unity from which they originate, if genders merge and identify themselves by going back to the primitive simplicity, then perfections also disappear, and this indistinct absolute can no longer reunite them. It then becomes the cause of the perfections that its manifestations produce, but it is a cause distinct from the effect that cannot be brought back into it without annihilating it.

Moreover, if we admit that all perfections can be found united in one being, we must also believe that its perfection is infinite. But, since perfection is a quality that presupposes the substance of which it is a quality, it follows that if the quality of being is infinite, its substance is also infinite. Therefore, the spiritual substance of God is infinite.

But if God is infinite, the world composed of material substance cannot exist because where material substance would begin, the spiritual substance of God would end. God would then have a limit and would no longer be infinite.

Thus, equally, the human spirit could not exist. Because it is composed of a spiritual substance that, however, is imperfect, it does not have the fullness of being which is only of the Creator. But then, where the imperfect spiritual substance begins, the perfect spiritual substance would cease, that is, God would be limited a second time. But this is impossible because God is infinite, and the infinite is what has everything in it and outside of which, there is nothing. Therefore, either the world and the human spirit exist in God, are his different manifestations, his distinct emanations in form, but equal in substance, and then, there is no duality of substances, everything is God, and we and the world are in it, are a part of it, but God becomes the immanent God of pantheism, which Zòffoli, as a Christian, certainly will not accept; or else, God is transcendent, but then, he cannot create other substances outside of himself that would limit his infinity. In that case, there is only God, infinite and eternal, and the world and the human spirit do not exist.

To this argument of mine, Zòffoli replied, "God

is the infinite, the absolute, the necessary. The world is a finite reality, if it were infinite, then it would not exist because two infinities exclude each other. But since the world is finite, there is no incompatibility between the two. Let's assume two straight lines: the first does not circumscribe the length of the other; they are not contradictory; the finite does not limit the infinite, which is inexhaustible; the two lines remain distinct. An example: the power of the officer does not limit that of the king. The officer is not opposed to the king, who remains king, and yet, the king is one thing, and the officer is another. Let us conceive of the finite world and the infinite God."

But it is not so, Theologian Zòffoli. The two lines both unfold in the space in which they are both contained. One follows space to infinity; the other stops at a certain point. The second does not limit the first but remains distinct from it because both always remain separate in the same space. But if the finite line were outside of space, then it would limit both this and the infinite line that extends infinitely with it.

The authority of the officer does not limit that of the king because it operates within the realm of the king's authority. If it were to develop outside of this realm, then it would indeed limit the authority of the king, which would cease at the point where the authority of the officer begins.

Zòffoli also stated, as I transcribe from his speech that I have stenographed here,

Martucci says, *How do you establish what is good and what is evil? You say that only God is good, but what is goodness? What is love? What is justice?"* And I answer, *Good and evil do not exist in themselves, but it is man who judges good or evil according to his beliefs. Protagoras says, 'Man is the measure of all things.'* But I reply to Martucci, How do we establish what is good and evil? We arrive at these concepts through induction, intuition, experience, and with that, we can establish phenomena, construct science, and judge men and history. Is it true that good and evil are creations of man? In this case, these concepts have no absolute value; what is good seems good to me and not to another, and in this way, we tie our hands. So how can Martucci blame God for being evil, unjust, if God thought he was doing good as he did? How can we judge the actions of the priests? We talk about the injustice of the Inquisition, but how can we judge if we do not know what is good and what is evil? Everyone can do what suits them.

In fact, I do not believe in the existence of morality, justice, duty, and all those other lies invented by some men to better deceive and oppress others without fear of encountering resistance. I think, with Stirner and Nietzsche, that the essence of man is egoism, which can only be satisfied by strength (meaning not only physical but also intellectual strength).

There is no qualitative hierarchy in nature among

ENZO MARTUCCI

vital manifestations, but they are all equivalent because they are all necessary, both the manifestations that give life and the others that produce death, from which new life arises. Good and evil do not exist in themselves; it is man who judges everything to be good or bad, but each person judges in their own way, differently from others. Therefore, my good is your evil, and your evil is my good. Everyone does what they believe; if the actions of others offend my feelings or interests, I can react by defending myself, but I cannot judge and condemn my opponents: I cannot say that they should not have done what they did.

So I neither blame nor condemn God if, to satisfy a whim, He has taken me from nothingness and thrown me into the arms of pain. I do not reproach Him for His actions, for the punishment inflicted on Adam, who had used the freedom granted to him by God himself and had chosen as he pleased. I do not judge Him for the undeserved suffering decreed against Adam's innocent descendants, for the flood in which men and beasts drowned, for the ordered massacre of the firstborn children of the Egyptians. I do not criticize Him for the command given to Moses to have the worshippers of the golden calf slaughtered by the Levites and for the plague sent to the Jews that David had wanted to census. If God, for His selfishness, wanted to do so, He did well to act in this way. Similarly, I do not judge the priests; I do not condemn them; I do not reproach the Inquisition for the stakes on which millions of heretics were burned alive. If the inquisitors, for their selfishness as fanatics or for the protection of their material interests, believed it was good to eliminate all enemies of the Catholic faith or all those who did not want to endure the tyranny or exploitation of the church, they could not act otherwise.

But in this case, if God is not a loving father and thinks only of Himself, if the church is not a tender mother but only cares about its own benefit, sacrificing its own children when it is advantageous, then we humans must not sacrifice our selfishness at the feet of God and the church, we must not be more fearful and devoted servants, and we must no longer accept the law of God and His representatives on Earth. Instead, we must rebel to regain the freedom that allows each of us to live as we please. Therefore, when I recall the ferocity of the biblical god and the misdeeds of the priests, it is not to condemn them in the name of a moral norm in which I do not believe, but it is to unmask the hypocrisy of the church, which wants us to believe that the Heavenly Father is merciful and compassionate, that the priests are good and altruistic, and that, therefore, we must respect them, love them, and obey the just discipline they dictate.

Selfishness against selfishness: if the church, for its own interest, imposed its tyranny on us and maintained it by all means, we, for our own interest, can rise up and break the chains, using all means. This is the meaning of my criticism, esteemed theologian. Not an ethical judgment but a utilitarian evaluation.

Referring then to the cosmological argument of Thomas Aquinas, which I briefly examined, Zòffoli endeavored to demonstrate that the insufficient must come from the sufficient, the finite from the infinite, the movement from the unmoved mover, which is outside and behind things. The world is finite; therefore, it is the work of an infinite god.

But, dear friar, the infinite cannot create the finite outside of itself; otherwise, it limits itself. It can create within itself, but then it creates the infinite because an infinite cause can only correspond to an infinite effect. If God is infinite, who is the unity of everything that is explained in the universe, then the universe is also infinite, which is nothing but the manifestation of the divine essence. Infinite perfection must manifest itself through an infinity of beings and worlds. But this is the philosophy of Giordano Bruno, for whom the cause, which is the infinite unity considered as opposed to the world that springs from it, is also the principle that is the same unity considered as immanent in the world.

However, for Thomas Aquinas, the cause is transcendent, producing the effect outside of itself. The world is not emanated—it is not the manifestation of divinity—but it is created by God, who remains separate from it, and then either the infinite cause produces an infinite effect, but, in this case, two infinities cannot coexist, or the infinite cause generates a finite effect, and there is a contradiction. Moreover, the finite effect would limit the infinity of the cause. God would be limited by the world that he would have created outside of himself.

Regarding the criticism I made of Aquinas'

theological or teleological argument, Zòffoli observed,

> According to St. Thomas, we have finality in nature. Animals do not think, they are not free, and then there is another being that has ordered them. For example, the clock does not think but tells time. If it does not depend on man, it must depend on another, divine being. Martucci says that there is order and disorder in nature, but I respond that order is more normal than disorder.
>
> In all of us, there is order; nature tends towards order, there is no chaos in it but laws and purpose.

The theologian spoke thus. But he forgot that in nature, order and disorder stand side by side, equally necessary. Next to every rule is an exception; next to every law, abnormality appears. For nature, they have equal value: both are necessary. Life and death, creation and dissolution, harmony and chaos, normality and abnormality are indispensable to nature because it is essential for it to manifest itself in different and opposing ways. How can it be said, then, that nature tends more towards one than the other? More towards order than disorder?

"An order and a judgment of things according to their value," I wrote in my book *Più oltre*,[15] "is only dreamed by the limitation of human thought, which attributes to the world its own purposes."

---

15   Enzo Martucci, *Più oltre* (Pistoia), 1947).

Furthermore, even if it could be shown that nature tends towards a purpose, as Kant observed, this would prove the existence of the Demiurge, not the transcendent God. God would act on things not as a foreign force but as the artisan who would push everything from within to preserve and order themselves better and to realize a superior harmony.

Zòffoli finally added, "The conclusion of Martucci's speech was this: *Mine is not the position of the atheist, not that of the agnostic, but that of the free man who wants to be without God and without a master.* But I ask if this attitude can be said of a thinker or one who has let himself be carried away by passion. I say this is not admissible in a serious person because if the existence of God were proven to him, he should do nothing but kneel and worship Him."

In fact, after refuting all the proofs of the existence of God, even those of Kant and Pascal, which Zòffoli refused to discuss on the pretext that they are not accepted by Catholic philosophy, I concluded the senses do not perceive God; reason does not prove it to me but rather attests to the weakness of the arguments with which theologians try to prove it. However, I know that the senses do not make me aware of reality, I know that human reason is limited, and, therefore, I also admit that God could exist, even if it appears impossible to me. But even if He existed and suddenly revealed Himself to me, I would have to declare to Him that I would not recognize His authority or submit to it.

According to Zòffoli, I should kneel down and

worship. But why? Maybe because God is my creator? But did I ask Him to bring me out of nothingness? And if He brought me into being by His own will, why did He condemn me to the condition of a slave who must always obey the law imposed by the Divine Master if He wants to avoid more terrible punishments?

Furthermore, even by obeying, I am not freed from pain. It continues to torment me. It is inseparable from life. And why did God create the pain that eternally torments us?

Saint Augustine asserts that pain comes from the evil that is within us. But this evil is not a reality but a privation, a deficiency of the only reality that is good, perfection. God creates us good, perfect like him. But he does not give us all his goodness, all his perfection; otherwise, we humans would be equal to God, we would be many gods, and it would become impossible to distinguish between the Creator and his creatures. Therefore, that bit of goodness, of perfection, that is lacking in us constitutes evil, human imperfection.

But why didn't God create us equal to Him: why didn't He make us gods? Maybe because He didn't want to share the governance of the universe with us and intended to remain the sole despot? Then why didn't God refrain from creating? Because His goodness did not resist the impulse that urged Him to manifest Himself by limiting Himself? Against God, therefore, I would oppose my revolt. And even if He unleashed all the thunderbolts of His wrath upon me, He could not bend my will, as He did not bend that of Prometheus, chained to the rock of Caucasus, or that of Capaneus, lying under the rain of fire.

This frenzied revolt, this paroxysmal desire for freedom that drives the anarchic individual to rebel against every divine or human authority and to break every religious, ethical, and legal restraint, would produce, in its generalization, the disintegration of society and the triumph of the *bellum omnium contra omnes*.[16]

So said Zòffoli, but I oppose him, saying that a balance between individual selfishness is possible because it is determined in certain cases by the mutual benefit that people find in agreement and in other cases by the resistance that any attack encounters when everyone is fiercely defending their own personality.

Zòffoli also affirmed the existence of the absolute and described it in detail, demonstrating the vanity of theology, which not only claims to have found this absolute but also asserts that it knows it thoroughly and knows that it is composed of a spiritual substance endowed with the attributes of infinity, eternity, indivisibility, etc. All theologians agree in defining God in the same way, while philosophers, even when they believe they have discovered the absolute, each conceive of it in their own way. Philosophy is not yet satisfied: it does not definitively accept any of these absolutes and continues the

---

16   "A war of all against all." (Ed.)

eternal search, destined to never find complete satisfaction. The philosophical activity can be considered useless, and one can pass, as Comte hoped, from attempting to understand the ultra-phenomenal to the observation and study of the phenomenal. That is, one can renounce metaphysics and dedicate oneself only to science. But as long as philosophy exists, it will always pursue the phantom of the absolute, and at the moment when one philosopher believes he has reached it, another will demonstrate to him that it is not that, and the race will resume.

On the other hand, theologians do not need to run. They believe they have found the absolute, and all agree in conceiving it equally because they all see it with the same eyes. And yet, their absolute is neither perceptible nor understandable. And to these gentlemen, I say that I do not know whether the absolute exists or not, but I know that I can never know it. I am a skeptic—I doubt everything—but since, in order to live, I must accept a reality, then I accept and treat the appearance as such, even though I know that it may not be reality. But even if I were given the opportunity to know the absolute and to find out that it is precisely what you say, namely, God the Almighty Father, Creator of Heaven and Earth, I would not kneel at His feet but would stand straighter than ever.

If the various Zòffolis love bowing, I prefer pride. If the sheep desire the shepherd, I aspire to freedom. And on the banner of my rebellion, I have written, for thirty years, with the blood of my veins, the motto that expresses the supreme necessity of my tormented soul—*frangar, non flectar.*[17]

---

17   "I will break, but I will not bend." (Ed.)

DOES JUSTICE EXIST?

Professor Decio Conti (what is his intellectual and political position?) believes in the existence of justice. And when I asked him to explain what it is, he replied, "Justice is an idea that humans have accepted since ancient times, which has been passed down from generation to generation and has become fixed in the human mind, exerting its influence on our thinking and conduct."

Very well! Conti is right. All or almost all men have accepted, since the earliest times, the idea of justice. However, everyone has always interpreted it in their own way. Each people and each class, each group and each individual, has had its own conception of justice, different from that of other peoples and classes, other groups and other individuals.

The Romans believed it was just to conquer the lands of the barbarians and forcibly impose their civilization upon them. The barbarians believed it was just to repel the invader, preserve their freedom, and reject civilization. The Crusaders believed they were serving justice by liberating the Holy Sepulchre and driving the Turks out of Jerusalem. The Turks claimed that justice was on their side because they were defending the true faith and resisting the aggression of the Westerners. Modern socialists declare themselves to be the only champions of equity, aiming to destroy borders and unite peoples in a unified humanity. Nationalists assert that their ideal is just, which advocates for independence for every people and their right to excel, by any means, over others. The austere family father claims that justice inspires him when he tries to prevent his young and inexperienced daughter from succumbing to the seducer's temptations and the perdition that lies therein. The daughter thinks it is fair that she should be able to dispose of her body as she wishes and give it to the man she loves, in contravention of her father's prohibition.

It is clear, therefore, that there is not a single, eternal, and universal justice, but there are many different and opposing justices.

Which of these will be the true one?

If we had Platonic Hyperuranian realms, and humans could fix their eyes on it and see the transcendent idea of justice, the absolute and perfect model, then it would be easy to establish that among the various human conceptions of justice, the true one is the one that resembles the model. But since the Hyperuranian realm does not exist, the model is missing, and the consequence is that all different and opposing ideas of justice are all true or all false, or they are all neither true nor false. Therefore, they are all equivalent.

However, although different, these various conceptions share the claim to demand sacrifice from the individual. Every notion of justice requires the self to be sacrificed on its altar.

The Roman must endure the hardships and dangers of war and risk ending up in the Teutoburg Forest, under the spears of the primitives. The barbarian is forced to expose himself to the retaliation of the conquerors and the fate of Vercingetorix. The Crusader is obliged to abandon his homeland, family, and interests to face the threat posed by Saladin. The Turk must face the wrath of Richard the Lionheart and his ruthless warriors. The socialist challenges the galley, poverty, and persecution of capitalist society. The nationalist offers his life in the struggle against the foreigner and knows that he will end up in prison if socialism prevails. The head of the family, to prevent the corruption of his daughter, torments his soul and imposes serious financial sacrifices to keep her in school or pay servants to watch over her. The daughter runs the risk of ending up on the streets or in the brothel, where she will contract syphilis, contempt, and misery.

Every conception of justice, therefore, requires from the individual who accepts it submission to a duty that sacrifices man. But what does justice give in return to the sacrificed?

A reward: the satisfaction of having acted morally, of having avoided the penalty of remorse, or of having earned the esteem of others and having

ENZO MARTUCCI

become pleasing to God or humanity.

Therefore, justice demands a sacrifice from the individual that it compensates with a reward.

But in the same way, self-interest behaves as well. It tells me, *If you want the joy of getting rich, you have to expose yourself to the strain of work or the dangers of theft. If you want to possess a beautiful woman, you have to ruin yourself financially for her or face the gun of the jealous husband. If you desire to conquer glory, you have to obtain it by consuming your health on books and enduring the slanders and treacheries of the envious. If you aspire to crown your ambition with dictatorial power, resign yourself to endure struggles, setbacks, risks, and mental anguish.*

Therefore, just like justice, self-interest conditions the reward it promises us with the sacrifice it demands. But if both self-interest and justice demand my pain in exchange for pleasure (spiritual or material), then I must consider them equivalent and find no reason to consider justice superior to self-interest.

One might say, *If I do not serve justice, if I do not submit to duty, I will be exposed to the torment of remorse that torments the soul. But equally, if I neglect self-interest, if I do not pay attention to the benefits, I may suffer, later on, the agony of moral pains no less than the pains that torment an honest man who has sinned.*

"If the feeling of duty," writes Ferrari,

> makes those who resist it feel ashamed, if it gnaws at them with remorse, even self-interest brings

with it a legion of regrets and pains; it punishes us with its remorse and uses shame to make us obey. Look at the facts: that girl moans, weighed down by her virginity; that king is afflicted, having committed the terror of being just; that general is sorrowful because he was not treacherous; that minister is unhappy, wishing he had violated his oath. Tito was sad on the day he was not beneficent; the leader Gabrino Fondulo died in despair for not having killed the pope and the emperor when he had hosted them in Cremona. Should we imitate Tito or the leader? Logic forbids us to answer. In the face of logic, the characters of duty and interest are filial. Like duty, interest changes, gives way to habit, education, and circumstances; it varies with customs, climate, and civilization. Sometimes, interest is doubtful, uncertain, reflective; these are the same phenomena as duty. In the Middle Ages, it invoked the casuistry of the church and that of chivalry; it demands the study of jurisprudence and the decisions of the courts everywhere. Interest can at least partially disappear: we can become insensitive to the most attractive pleasures, can happily do without them; in love, one being lives in the other, and interest suspends the reign of interest. The same phenomenon is reproduced in duty: remorse disappears with the habit of the crime; entire nations can forget the first principles of humanity; in antiquity, the whole human race consecrated the injustice of slavery; the

ENZO MARTUCCI

same injustice is still consecrated in the vastest regions of the globe. There, man is a machine; he is flogged, wounded, killed; the laws of justice remain suspended in the very sanctuary of conscience, those of modesty are vain; the slave has no gender to seduce the free woman nor to make her ashamed. How will we force the perverted man to follow a feeling he does not have?

The two institutions of interest and duty are reduced to two impulses, two forces; if there is no reason to prefer one to the other, the choice will be dictated by the intensity of the forces. Logic will give way to mechanics. Therefore, the stronger impulse will have the right to take us with it; therefore, the action, the necessary result of the stronger impulse, will always be just; therefore, it will be just to be unjust when the fatalism of selfishness prevails over the force of duty. Do not ask whether to honor the virtuous or the unjust, whether to imitate Seneca or Nero. The question no longer makes sense; be what you are, value what succeeds: the fact is the right.[18]

We do not have, therefore, a valid reason to consider justice superior to interest and to prefer the former over the latter in choice. Like interest, pagan justice, Christian justice, socialist justice, and nationalist justice demand sacrifice from the individual that they reward with a benefit, and they sanction the remorse of the deserter. Therefore, all justices have the

18   Giuseppe Ferrari, *Philosophy of the Revolution*.

same characteristics of usefulness. Why, then, should I consider them better than this usefulness?

But Kant's justice requires sacrifice without offering any reward. I must do good for the sake of good; I must not have any other aim than justice. If I were to do good in order to obtain an advantage, to have inner satisfaction, to avoid the pain of remorse, to make myself worthy of Paradise in the afterlife, to gain the esteem of men, or to obtain a sentimental or material pleasure, then my action would be egoistic; its aim would be myself, not justice, and I would not have acted morally. Instead, I must act disinterestedly, against the impulses of sentiment and selfishness, to conform to the moral law that I find in my reason and that imposes on my will a command that reason recognizes as universal and unconditional.

"You must; therefore, you can," says Kant. Therefore, I can go against my interests and my tendencies only because the moral law requires me to do so.

But contrary to what Kant affirms, the same moral law that all reasons recognize as necessary and just cannot be found in all human reasons. Instead, each reason creates its own morality that is in conflict with the morals created by other reasons. And each reason generates its own ethics under the influence of the feelings, needs, interests, and passions that prevail in the individual. Therefore, disinterested action, good for the sake of good, duty for duty's sake, is never encountered in human conduct.

According to Kant, reason can never demonstrate

ENZO MARTUCCI

to any man that it is rational to offend justice or violate the freedom of other human beings. But why couldn't it? Kant responds that it is necessary to respect the freedom of others. "But why," Ferrari asks,

should I respect the person, the freedom of my fellow human beings? My freedom is my interest; their freedom limits it; by respecting my freedom, I am happy, but by respecting the freedom of my fellow human beings, I am sacrificing myself. Therefore, I will do as I please, and too bad for those who suffer. I only know myself, and the conflict between my freedom and that of my fellow human beings reproduces, without resolving, the dilemma of good and evil. Kant claims to force me to do my duty out of the necessity of being consistent; he asks me if I want to vilify the freedom that I claim, if I want to refuse to others what I demand for myself. Yes, of course; if my freedom is a principle, I want to be absolutely free, and I cannot be accused of contradiction by refusing to respect the freedom in others that I demand for myself. The contradiction would occur if it fell on the same object, if I were intent on claiming and rejecting my own freedom; then, to be logical, I would be forced to choose to be free or a slave, persecutor or victim. But by violating justice, I demand freedom for myself and servitude for others, and putting duty aside, I remain logically faithful to the principle of my own independence. There is nothing more natural.

Thus, Ferrari demonstrates to us the impossibility of justice based on logic. However, he also ends up recognizing justice founded on human nature.

For him, duty is determined by usefulness because there is in us an inexplicable but real impulse that drives us to sacrifice certain particular interests to the natural and general interest in which personal interest is truly and completely realized. This impulse, as it unfolds, varies infinitely, creates the most diverse morals, drives Christ to sacrifice himself for the redemption of all humanity and Achilles to fight and suffer to obtain the triumph of the Greeks over the Trojans. It is revealed in the honest person who works for the community, in the idealist who struggles and suffers for the liberation of the people, in the wrongdoer who allows himself to be thrown into jail rather than betray his companions or even give up everything to consummate the crime. The general interest requires the abnegation of the individual who participates in it, and this abnegation reaches the holy contradiction of the complete sacrifice of interest.

The morality of Ferrari is nothing but the utilitarian morality of Bentham revised and corrected. Does the impulse for sacrifice truly exist in all men? Are there not many men who are not inclined to sacrifice themselves for others or even for themselves, content with little rather than striving for much that they could not attain without renunciation and danger? And among those who are willing to sacrifice themselves, is this tendency sometimes reconcilable

ENZO MARTUCCI

with the general interest but at other times in contrast to the interest of their fellow men?

In nature, there is an instinct that drives us to mutual support, and that Kropotkin has studied so well, but there is also an inclination that drives us to war, to the struggle for existence. It is true that Darwin has shown that this struggle is more severe between different species than between individuals belonging to the same species. However, it also exists within the same species, and we feel that in certain cases, we can realize our personal interest in the general interest, but in certain other cases, we realize that our own interest can only be satisfied at the expense of others.

We are, at the same time, social and antisocial, generous and perverse. How can we then claim that the strongest natural tendency is the one that drives us to feel our individual benefit in the benefit of all? The delinquent who sacrifices himself not to denounce his companions seeks, at another moment, to defraud them of the products of the theft committed together. He exposes himself to their revenge, runs the risk of giving and receiving stabbings, but all this he does for an interest that conflicts with that of others. The honest worker who sweats in the field or in the factory, if he manages to acquire a small property, exploits his workers as the boss exploited him. The idealist who has suffered for so many years to liberate humanity can finally, when he has achieved his goal, become a tyrant and oppress the same humanity that he had wanted to free before.

Therefore, it is not possible to found justice on

natural tendencies that are varied and contradictory.

The conclusion is therefore that justice, invariable and universal, does not exist. The different and opposing notions of justice have the same characteristics of self-interest, and there is no logical reason to prefer one over the other. A justice of selflessness cannot exist, just as a justice created by natural spontaneity cannot exist.

Therefore, justice does not exist.

INDIVIDUALIST AMORALISM

Is individualist anarchism reconcilable with morality? E. Armand believes so and writes, "One can build a morality that is in no way inferior to the strictest moral codes and not abandon any of one's individualism pushed to the extreme."

I, on the other hand, believe that individualist anarchism must necessarily be amoralistic precisely because it cannot agree with any morality.

At this point, I think it's important to specify that by morality, I don't mean the subjective judgment of "what I should do and what I shouldn't do" because such judgment varies from individual to individual, and even within the same individual, as their feelings, passions, needs, and ideas change or evolve. Instead, morality is the superior norm, the absolute law, the peremptory order that imposes on everyone what they must always do and what they are always bound not to do.

Stirner has the same conception of morality as me. "People are at pains," he writes in *The Ego and* to distinguish law from arbitrary orders, from an ordinance: the former comes from a duly entitled authority. But a law over human action (ethical law, State law, etc.) is always a *declaration of will*, and so an order. Yes, even if I myself gave myself the law, it would yet be only my order, to which in the next moment I can refuse obedience. One may well enough declare what he will put up with, and so deprecate the opposite by a law, making known that in the contrary case he will treat the transgressor as his enemy; but no one has any business to command *my* actions, to say what course I shall pursue and set up a code to govern it. I must put up with it that he treats me as his enemy, but never that he makes free with me as his *creature*, and that he makes *his* reason, or even unreason, my plumb-line.[19]

Therefore, if the rule of conduct is imposed on me by others, I must rebel against this imposition because I want to live my life in my own way and not as the neighbors—who have different feelings, interests, opinions, and needs than mine—dictate. And if the rule of conduct is imposed on me by myself, with my reason, I can later repudiate it when my reason, thinking differently under the influence of changed feelings and interests, shows me the absurdity of the rule that had previously been given to me. Or I

---

19   Max Stirner: *The Ego and His Own.*

can break the rule still accepted by my reason if, at a certain moment, my instincts and feelings burst out against it and momentarily take over in me.

If instead I continue to obey the norm even when my reason condemns it or when I feel it in too sharp a contrast with my instinctive and sentimental needs, then it means that I consider it superior to myself, consider it sacred, and attribute to it an objective reality, a value independent of me. But in this case, I am a slave to a fantasy, a victim of suggestion.

A free individual cannot, therefore, commit to following a single rule of conduct for their entire life, and it is absurd to expect them to always conform to the same norm and even more absurd and tyrannical is to want all of humanity to accept and always follow this one law. Every morality—whether Confucian or Buddhist, Mosaic or Socratic, Christian or Islamic, Kantian or utilitarian, humanitarian or nationalist— always declares that it is universal, the true morality, that is, the legitimate rule that all men, in all times and in all places, must recognize and practice. But this demand of every morality is simply insane because that spiritual unity that Kant considered possible in the future does not exist and will never exist. In fact, there is not one reason that reasons equally in all men, but there are many reasons that reason differently in the various individuals who have different needs, interests, and tastes. Consequently, there are always many who do not accept that rule of conduct, not recognizing it as useful or just. And among those who do accept it, disagreements immediately arise about how to interpret the norm.

Let us take, for example, the Christian rule "Do unto others as you would have them do unto you." The first Christians understood it in this way: "Never, under any circumstances, not even in legitimate defense, should you do to others what you would not want done to you." And since they would not want to suffer violence, they did not use it even against the Roman soldiers who arrested them to throw them to the beasts. But other Christians who came later, other Christians who were also sincere and in good faith, explained the maxim as follows: "Do not do unto others what you would not have them do unto you, but react with violence to those who use violence to unjustly oppress you."

So much so that the Albigenses and the Waldenses fell, with weapons in hand, fighting against the Catholic Crusaders who attacked and massacred them.

Among the Catholics, even among those who aspired to the absolute triumph of the church out of fervent fanaticism and not for the sole purpose of earthly domination, the rule was interpreted in this other way: "Do not do unto others what you would not have them do unto you, but use violence, torture, and fire against the heretics who, even if they do not physically attack you, propagate theories contrary to your faith." Therefore, individuals who, like Cardinal Federico Borromeo, were just and humane in their private lives showed themselves to be inexorable and ferocious as inquisitors.

It is clear, therefore, that every rule of conduct can be subject to different interpretations that lead individuals to opposite practices in life. Only when, at a certain time and in a certain place, some people manage to impose their interpretation on others by physical force or persuasion, then the triumph of a single morality is achieved, equally understood and followed by everyone. But this triumph is nothing but a frightful tyranny under which men writhe, made slaves and forced to obey the sacred law and to think and act in the same way. And against such a chain, the free individual can only oppose the taut bow of his rebellion.

Armand will say that my criticisms are well-directed towards absolute morality but not towards the morality that can be followed by an individualist, that is, towards relative morality that is moral only for those who recognize it as useful and for the time when they choose to follow it. But I will reply that if morality is such, it always claims to be absolute, to possess the character of necessity and universality, and, therefore, to be valid as a uniform rule of conduct for men in every era and in every country. Otherwise, it is not a law, it is not morality, but a personal judgment that varies from one person to another and that I can change in myself when I want. And so I return, with Protagoras, to "the measure of all things" and, with Stirner, to the "unique."

The anarchist individualist feels that nothing is above his self and rebels against all discipline and authority, divine or human. He does not recognize any morality, and even when he indulges in feelings of love, friendship, sociability, he does so for his own natural needs, for his own selfish satisfaction, because he likes to do so. When he feels the need to rise up and fight against other men, he does not hesitate for a moment to follow this different tendency, but never, under any circumstances, does the anarchist individualist submit to a common rule of conduct, valid for everyone, forever, that is, to the rule of the herd.

The above writing appeared in French in the March 1949 issue of the magazine *L'Unique* published by E. Armand in Orleans. In the same issue, Armand responded with an article titled "My response to Enzo Martucci." He began by asserting that in order to fully understand Stirner and his work, it is necessary to place them in the era in which he lived and wrote. He added that "we cannot ignore the situation in which Germany found itself at the time, shaken by criticism in religious matters and aspirations towards political freedom that would lead to the German revolution of 1848. Therefore, to fully understand *L'Unique*, it is necessary to neglect the part dedicated to history, which is weak anyway, to focus on everything that smells like pamphlets and controversy, and never lose sight of the fact that it is the liberal bourgeoisie of the time and its spokesmen that our author attacks throughout his book."

All of this, as Armand observes, is true in terms of the form of Stirner's work, and it is important to keep this in mind to better understand why Stirner adopted a certain tone and used certain arguments and why he particularly polemicized with liberal theorists. But it has nothing to do with the substance of *The Ego and His Own*. Because the substance of the book, from the first to the last word, asserts the natural need of the individual—who has not yet been emasculated by social influence—to be himself, to remain distinct, unique, different from others, with his own original way of feeling, thinking, and acting. And this need erupts, with an unstoppable surge of revolt, against the efforts that society has been making for millennia to level and emasculate all individuals, imposing certain beliefs, dogmas, and rules that lead to the most absolute conformity and the transformation of men into so many similar puppets who march obediently in rank, marking time with every order of the corporal.

Now the need for individuality, for the uniqueness of anarchic life in which the self, free from any religious, moral, and legal restraint, can satisfy, to the extent of its powers, all its egoistic impulses and personal tendencies, this genuine, primordial need, tenaciously rooted in our nature, has always been felt by the refractory, the unruly, the unbridled, in every time, in every place, in every society. It did not arise because of the particular spiritual, political, and economic conditions of Germany in 1840 nor from the need to counter the arguments of bourgeois philosophers. Instead, this need is eternal because it is natural, instinctive. Some men become conscious of it and justify it with reason, like Stirner; others feel it and follow the impulses it arouses, even if they cannot demonstrate to themselves and to others the legitimacy of their feelings and conduct. But the need is always real and reacts to the depressing influence of established society that seeks to herd individuals together, in every era and in every country: in the Babylon of Hammurabi and the Persia of Darius, in the Sparta of Lycurgus and the Athens of Solon, in the Rome of Cato and the Empire of Augustus, in the Byzantium of Justinian and the France of Charlemagne, in the Paris of Robespierre and the Russia of Stalin.

Armand is, therefore, wrong when he tries to reduce Stirnerism to the narrow limits of a philosophy produced by certain contingent interests manifested at a certain moment in history and in a given place. Stirnerism is the theorization of an eternal, natural, profound need that was felt even thousands of years before Stirner was born and that will cease with the end of the human species.

But such an interpretation of Stirnerism leads to the acceptance of natural life and the negation not only of religion and the state but also of all education, all morality, and every restraint that stifles instinct and egoism. Armand, on the other hand, despite professing to be an individualist anarchist, aspires to a cultured, composed, and correct life, always controlled by reason and never at the mercy of caprice and impulse. He repeats, with pleasure, Proudhon's aphorism "liberty is the mother of order" and does

ENZO MARTUCCI

not realize that he is saying, with Proudhon, utter nonsense. Liberty is, equally, the mother of both order and disorder, both of which are found in nature and are both necessary for nature and for humans, who find, in certain moments, the best way to assert themselves and enjoy in the regularity of the harmonious relationships maintained with their fellow beings, and in certain other moments, they satisfy and enjoy themselves through instability, risk, struggle, chaotic relationships with other individuals, or by distancing themselves from them. And since in liberty, humans live according to their natural tendencies precisely because there is no authority that forces them to live differently than they feel, it follows that both order and disorder are fully realized in liberty.

Armand's Stirner is a diluted Stirner who goes hand in hand with Proudhon, with Tucker, even with Tolstoy. Nor does Armand only capture the part of *The Ego and His Own* that demonstrates the possibility for individual egoism to be satisfied through free understanding with other egoisms, but he neglects the other part, in which Stirner argues that certain goods, spiritual or material, cannot be obtained except by conquering them, that is, by fighting.

Armand reduces everything to the association of egoists in Stirner's philosophy but then argues that he and his followers support a union that is consistent with Stirner's association. However, even this is not true.

In fact, Stirner admits that in order to satisfy one's own egoism, which is the driving force of one's personality, the individual must—depending on the situation—either contend with other individuals or come to an understanding and collaborate with them. In the latter case, one associates freely. Association takes away certain freedoms, such as the freedom to attack or exploit one's companions, to reduce them to slavery, etc., but, in exchange, it grants other freedoms that one could not obtain alone or that would require greater effort to obtain. As long as it is convenient for me, everything is fine. I, says Stirner, do not aim for absolute freedom, which would lead me to free myself from everything, even life, even what gives me pleasure and that I want to keep. Instead, I seek the freedom to free myself from everything that stifles my egoism and prevents the satisfaction of my needs and the freedom to preserve everything that gives me joy and power. In a word, I do not aim for freedom as a religious ideal but for my freedom, that is, for the triumph of my personality.

If that personality, at a certain moment, finds association pleasant or useful, it associates. But as soon as the individual feels that association is no longer convenient for him because his needs, dispositions, or interests have changed, then he withdraws from the association and does as he pleases. If the companions hold me back when I want to leave—if they do not allow me to abandon them at any moment and impose duties on me that bind me to the associates and do not return my freedom until the associates want to give it back to me—then the association is transformed into organization, society, an entity that considers itself superior to me and regards me as its property, which it can do whatever it wants with. In this case, I am a slave; society is my master and stifles my egoism.

"You bring into a union your whole power, your competence," Stirner says.

> and *make yourself count*; in a society you are *employed*, with your working power; in the former you live egoistically, in the latter humanly, *i.e.* religiously, as a "member in the body of this Lord"; to a society you owe what you have, and are in duty bound to it, are—possessed by "social duties"; a union you utilize, and give it up undutifully and unfaithfully when you see no way to use it further. If a society is more than you, then it is more to you than yourself; a union is only your instrument, or the sword with which you sharpen and increase your natural force; the union exists for you and through you, the society conversely lays claim to you for itself and exists even without you; in short, the society is *sacred*, the union your own; the society consumes *you, you* consume the union.[20]

Now, the association that Armand wants to establish with his disciples is based on the principle *pas de repture unilaterale du pacte* (no unilateral breaking of the pact). Individuals unite for the satisfaction of certain needs—economic, sexual, spiritual, etc.,

---

20   Max Stirner: *The Ego and His Own*.

needs—and base their co-operation on a contract that cannot be revoked, at any moment, by only one of those who have accepted it first. Therefore, to withdraw from the association, I must obtain the consent of the others; if the members do not give me such consent, if they do not agree with me on the need to terminate the agreement, I must remain obligated to them. Thus, I depend on others; I cannot dispose of myself as I feel, as I want; I am bound irrevocably to my companions, and only because yesterday, driven by certain feelings and certain needs, I wanted to join, but today that, driven by other feelings and other needs, I want to separate, I can no longer do so. But this is not the Stirnerian association; it is, instead, the society that Stirner condemns. It is a society built on the same model as all societies that enslave the individual. And just as in the current world, the state sends me to jail or shoots me if I do not conform to its laws, so in Armand's society, the companions kill me if I try to dissolve the contract I had previously accepted.

In his parable "Le paragraphe XIII," Armand speaks to us of a young woman who promises eternal love to her lover but then abandons him when she realizes that the passion has vanished from her heart. The man still loves her, and in despair, he kills himself. The friends of the dead man kidnap the woman, bring her before their court, and say to her, "You had promised to love our comrade forever. You did not keep your promise and have thus caused his suicide. We, who were bound to him by a pact that committed us to defend each other, punish you, in his place, for the failure to keep your word." They then shoot her with their guns.

Armand advocates for a strict and absolute morality that imposes certain duties on individuals, such as restraining their feelings and instincts according to reason and will, keeping promises even when their heart disagrees, and not breaking contracts without the consent of partners. The individual who has accepted this morality must continue to conform to it, even if they feel the need to reject it due to their changing needs. If they break it and follow their spontaneity, their companions will kill them. Thus, this morality, like all moralities, becomes a heavy burden that oppresses the individual. It is one of those ghosts that produce our unhappiness and against which Stirner, the amoralist, rails.

Moreover, this morality, by trying to prove that it is the only true one that teaches men the best rule of conduct, tends to universalize itself and become the sole law for all humanity. It is, therefore, like all other moralities, Christian, Buddhist, Kantian, etc.

Armand, short of arguments, becomes angry and writes, "So if my friends and I find it suitable for our temperament, sensitivity, aspirations, and what constitutes our individuality to gather and live together, according to an ethic of austerity, a rigid self-discipline, that is our business. Neither Enzo Martucci nor anyone else has the right to meddle in our affairs."

Fine! Armand is right. He and his friends can live as they please, and no one should interfere with their affairs. Even monks have the right to live in their own way and associate to worship God. But even though Armand and the monks are free to live as they please, I have the right to criticize and can think and say that the monks make themselves slaves of God and that Armand and his disciples make themselves slaves of their morality. Therefore, being voluntary slaves, they are not anarchists, and they

have nothing in common with Stirner, the enemy of all slavery, the individualist *par excellence*.

Armand is a sympathetic figure of an idealist, who, at 77 years old, still spreads his theories. However, while I respect the man, I contradict the philosopher. I have contradicted him since 1925, and I believe that his Quakerish anarchy, or very close to Quakerism, is nothing but the latest disguise of Christian morality to perpetually keep the natural individual in chains.

ENZO MARTUCCI

THE HOLY FAMILY

The philosopher Giuseppe Ferrari considers the family as a fact that is not rationalized but naturally true.

"Logic dissolves the family," he writes. "Speak of marital fidelity? There are no laws for love. Speak of the duty of father and mother towards their children? Children are children of nature and not of man's will.[21] Speak of the duties of children towards their parents? Children owe nothing to their relatives, who generate them without thinking of anything but themselves. Love can be reversed, and logic cannot choose between health and illness, between the constitution and the dissolution of the family."

However, according to Ferrari, this is a product of natural revelation, a fact created by appearance, which is our only reality and does not explain or demonstrate the usefulness of the family but makes us feel that it is necessary.

---

21   By adopting the "Law of Hyginus", future children could, indeed, depend solely on the will of man. (See *L'occhio nell'alcova* [*The Eye in the Alcove*], published by us). (L'Ed.)

And here, I no longer agree with the positivist philosopher. Man does not instinctively feel the need for the family, which is not the fatal consequence of our natural inclinations but an institution artificially created by society to allow, as Morgan argued, individuals who had become owners after conquering migrations to leave their property to children who were certainly their own.

If the family were the necessary form in which man satisfies his sexual needs, we should find it at the origins of our species. Instead, ethnology has revealed to us, through the observations and studies of Morgan, Bachofen, McLennan, Lubbock, and others, that in early human nuclei, there was promiscuity. In these groups, everything was shared among individuals driven to association by a natural instinct or a need for cooperation and help acquired during the glacial period and transmitted by inheritance to descendants. The products of hunting, fishing, and the collection of wild fruits belonged to everyone, and each person took from the pile according to their needs.

Even females were part of these primitive groups that practiced the system of anarchic communism. There were no leaders, no laws, natural sociability was the only bond that kept individuals together, but everyone followed their instincts, and females indiscriminately gave themselves to all males, satisfying their tendency for polyandry, and males possessed all females, one after the other, precisely because they were polygamous. Incest was also allowed, and the mother allowed herself to be taken by her son, and the brother mated with the sister. The young humanity felt a powerful erotic flame burning in its blood, of which our present old and exploited humanity only retains a poor spark.

If modern man is still polygamous and seeks a more acute voluptuous spasm in novelty and variety of pleasures, if contemporary woman is still polyandrous and passes, with the greatest delight, into the arms of many men when she has the courage to ignore morality, or when she believes she is protected by a well-kept secret, imagine what men and women of prehistoric times did, that is, those passionate, lustful, innocent beings, beyond good and evil, who could only find complete satisfaction of their lascivious fever in the most unrestrained promiscuity.

Morgan noted that in certain Pacific islands, children call the female who bore them "mother," and all adult males of the tribe "father." This custom shows that among those savages, promiscuity lasted until a recent time, so much so that even today, the infant calls any man "father" as in the time when paternity was unknown because all males possessed every female and, therefore, each of them could be the father of the children. Moreover, among the primitives of Australia, Melanesia, Polynesia, etc., there is a system of maternal descent that presupposes an original promiscuity.

For a very long time, promiscuity was the natural form in which sexual relationships took place throughout all of humanity. After centuries and centuries, with the birth of totemic beliefs, the original anarchic group transformed into an organized tribe divided into clans, which put the first brake on the wildness of natural freedom. Initially, incest was prohibited, and then sexual relationships were also forbidden among those who belonged to the same clan, meaning those who descended from a common progenitor, whose soul was imagined to be reincarnated in an animal worshipped as sacred. However, if the males of one clan could not mate with the females of the same clan, they collectively married the females of another clan and possessed them in common. This is what Lubbock calls communal marriage, which was nothing more than promiscuity that was just limited and disciplined by the rules of totemic worship.

Only millennia later, when agriculture was invented and many tribes joined together to abandon the barren lands on which they lived and seek out more fertile ones, we had conquering migrations. The most intelligent or cunning man who knew how to teach the masses how to overcome natural obstacles, who knew how to indicate the ford of a river, imagine the construction of a bridge, or devise the most effective defense against the attacks to which the migrants were exposed by the beasts and savages inhabiting the lands they crossed gained prestige, became the leader, and obtained the obedience that his companions would not have given him in any case before. When they reached the promised land, the leader directed his people in the conquest and

ENZO MARTUCCI

enslavement, by force, of the natives. He divided the conquered lands among his followers, each of whom became the owner not only of the piece of land but also of the vanquished people who lived on that piece of land. He himself transformed into the state that dictated the laws and regulated social relations between conquerors and conquered, between property owners and propertyless, all to the benefit of the former and to the detriment of the latter. Thus, natural freedom and primitive communism disappeared, and in their place were planted property and slavery, the state and the law.

The leader, who was worshipped as a god after his death, was believed to have an immortal soul endowed with supernatural power to protect his people, leading them from a totemic belief to a belief in a higher divinity (theism).

Collective marriage was replaced by individual marriage because individuals who had become property owners desired one or several women exclusively for themselves in order to have children who were certainly theirs and to whom they could leave their belongings upon death.

Therefore, the family was not founded by nature. Nature only founded promiscuity. The family was not the result of sexual tendency and individual love but of the economic organization of society, the institution of private property, and inheritance rights.[22]

22   Lewis Morgan, *Ancient Society*, and Friedrich Engels, *The Origin of the Family, Private Property and the State*.

It would disappear if the social forms that generated and maintained it disappeared.

Now let us examine the opposite hypothesis, which was supported by Aristotle up to Wundt, Westermark, Schopenhauer, Freud, and others: the family is a spontaneous product of nature. For Wundt, it is the monogamous family. For Schopenhauer, it is the polygamous family. But for both, humanity did not begin with the communist group where sexual promiscuity existed but with the exclusive union determined by man's need to have one or more women for himself alone and to dominate these women and the children they produce. From the agreement between families and their organization into a collective entity, community, society, and the state arose.

In this case, there would be a natural tendency that would drive man to form a family. But there would be another equally natural and instinctive tendency that would drive him to destroy it.

In males, does jealousy exist as an uncontrollable need to possess females or the female they have married, stolen, bought, or obtained exclusively for themselves? Well, if this need is not acquired, if it did not arise when man founded the family for economic, social, or religious reasons, then we can recognize that it exists as a natural given, but, at the same time, we must admit, because it is proven by evidence, that man naturally feels the need to mate with females who are not his. He imposes fidelity on his own women, but he tends towards polygamy. This is

ENZO MARTUCCI

true at all times and in all places, in the East and in the West, in antiquity and the Middle Ages, in the Renaissance and today.

Greek life is full of adulterers. The married citizen seeks out courtesans and also young men. The troubadour poetry extols love for another's woman. Modern times know only sexual infidelity.

Does the female, in turn, swear fidelity to the male she marries? Yes, but alongside the impulse that drives her to be only for one, the inclination immediately manifests itself that spurs her to grant herself to several males, to become Helen, Semiramis, Cleopatra, Theodora, Joanna of Naples, Catherine of Russia, to enjoy the different pleasures that different males can give her depending on their different ways of feeling, loving, and possessing a woman, either brutally or refinedly. One of these sexual ways may please this woman more than the others, and she feels anchored, with her senses and her heart, to the man who offers it to her. But she also feels the need to taste, even as an erotic diversion, the caresses of other males, and if among them, she finds one capable of impressing her more strongly, she breaks away from her old love and devotes herself, even with her soul, to the new passion. Therefore, the polyandrous tendency always coexists with jealousy and female exclusivity.

Do parents love their children with a purely sentimental transport that shuns any sexual relationship? Do children love their parents with an affection interwoven with respect and gratitude, deference and homage? Do siblings love sisters only with their hearts and not with their senses?

Ethnologists, regarding primitive peoples, and historians, regarding civilized peoples, answer such questions by saying that within the context of the family, both in its primordial and evolved forms, incestuous impulses have always struggled against the sentiments that tended to maintain chastity among relatives.

In ancient times, the mother would take the virginity of her son, the father would violate the daughter, and siblings would have sexual relations with each other. Incest was freely practiced by humans, just as it has always been practiced by animals. Even after religious and social prohibitions stifled it, it remained latent in our nature and resurfaced in the midst of civilization among diverse peoples.

The ancient Egyptians and Persians married their sisters. In the Avesta, it is written, "I approve and praise the holy marriage between relatives, which, of all present and future marriages, is the greatest, the best, the most beautiful, Ahuric, and Zoroastrian."

The Bible derives humanity from the union of Eve with her son Cain. The Incas of Peru married their sisters, just as the Egyptians did.

Aristippus, Cleanthes, Chrysippus, and other Greek philosophers maintained the legitimacy of incest. And they were not entirely wrong because the mother, sister, or daughter are females like any other, females who can ignite our senses, arouse passion in our hearts, and reproduce with us as with any male.

The evidence produced by some physiologists to demonstrate that degenerate beings are born from unions between consanguineous relatives has been refuted by the evidence produced by other physiologists, who have shown the opposite. Moreover, history teaches us that the Egyptians and Persians, born from incestuous unions, were physically strong enough to conquer neighboring peoples who did not practice incest and to found vast and powerful empires. They were also intellectually superior, to the point of creating two of the oldest and most splendid civilizations.

Freud claims that humanity began with polygamous families in which the jealous father prevented his young sons from having intercourse with his females.[23] But the sons formed an alliance, killed the father, and possessed his women in common, i.e., their mothers and sisters. However, the sons, who hated the father for preventing incestuous intercourse but simultaneously loved him as a guide and protector, repented of the crime committed after killing him and imposed, as atonement, the prohibition of further relations with their kin. Thus, morality and modesty were born, and from the adoration of the murdered father, whose soul was imagined to be reincarnated in the body of an animal, the first religious form arose: the totem cult.

Freud also argues that, as in the savage, the incestuous impulse is manifested powerfully in the child.

---

23   Sigmund Freud: *Totem and Taboo*.

According to the Austrian philosopher and scientist, erotic sensitivity does not arise in humans at puberty and is not localized in the genital organs alone but is also diffused in other organs where it has its centers and is active in the child who, by sucking the mother's breast, obtains nourishment and, after this, gratification of his libido by the pleasant rubbing that the nipple exerts on his labial mucosa. We are here in the first phase of sexual evolution, the oral phase. This is followed by the sadistic-pederastic phase, when the weaned child suffers from the lack of the breast and instinctively avenges himself by crushing insects or hurting other weak beings.

Moreover, he replaces the pleasure of the nipple with the rubbing that feces, in their passage, exert on his anal mucosa, another center of erotic sensitivity.

As the child grows older, he has an incestuous return towards the mother he enjoys touching her, hugging her, looking under her clothes, and hates the father, whom he intuits as a rival (the Oedipal phase).

Finally, after passing through the narcissistic phase, the boy reaches the endpoint of his sexual evolution because his genital organs, fully developed, make him capable of normal coitus and reproduction.

In the new needs that arise in this final stage, according to Freud, all the sexual needs that have manifested in previous stages remain absorbed. Only pathological motives (a strong impression and a nervous shock determined by the horror that the child, caught in the act and scolded, has felt for himself) can anchor a person, in adulthood, to the erotic needs of childhood.

However, contrary to Freud's conclusions, it is possible to believe that these needs, which are in our nature and arise from the need to satisfy libido with all the organs in which it permanently resides, continue to manifest themselves even in adults, not only for the pathological reasons advanced by Freud but also for normal causes. Only in this way can we explain that general tendency, more developed in some individuals than in others but present in all, that drives both males and females to desire to enjoy all erotic pleasures and to become intoxicated with all sensual delights. Only in this way can we understand why homosexuality, both female and male, has always been so widespread and is found—latent or pronounced—in the depths of everyone's nature, alongside the opposite heterosexual tendency.

Weininger, Ellis, and Maranon have interpreted this fact as the coexistence of both sexes in every individual. According to Maranon, both female and male hormones are found in the blood of each male and female, but in males, male hormones are present in greater numbers than female hormones, while in females, the opposite is true. However, the two sexes always appear together in the same individual, and when the dominant sex weakens under the influence of particular physical, psychological, or environmental conditions, then the opposite sex is revealed, giving rise to lesbian desires in women and pederastic tendencies in men.

There are also many individuals, who find themselves in a state that Maranon calls intersex, who have almost equal numbers of female and male hormones in their blood. Here, the two sexes are balanced, and the individual normally feels both heterosexual and homosexual stimuli, or only the latter.

Given the general tendency towards varied and intense lasciviousness, it must be deduced that while there are natural forces that push us towards forming families based on a permanent union between a man and a woman, there are also other natural forces that push men towards polygamy, women towards polyandry, both towards homosexuality, both towards incest, and, therefore, both towards the erotic freedom of promiscuity, in which only complete satisfaction of lust in its various forms is possible.

And if until now, the tendencies that drive us towards forming families have been the strongest because they are supported and reinforced by education, morality, and social institutions, in the future, in a world restored to the spontaneity of nature, the opposite tendencies could prove stronger, and we could return to the agamy and promiscuous and free love of the origins.

The female goes through the same stages of sexual evolution as the male. She begins by satisfying her lust by suckling at her mother's breast; then, weaned, she enjoys defecation and feels a vague impulse of lesbian nature that drives her towards other girls, just as boys, driven by a vague pederastic impulse, are drawn towards other boys. Until the age of seven, eight, or nine, children play at making love with children of the same sex. The game, kept hidden from adults who forbid it, leads to an incomplete homosexuality, more platonic than erotic, but it nevertheless shows that the tendency to mate with one's own sex is parallel to the inclination to mate with the opposite sex.

Once the heterosexual urge is manifested, the girl seeks out boys and feels an incestuous passion for her father, just as the boy approaches girls but is primarily attracted to the mother, in whom he instinctively recognizes the developed and complete woman.

With puberty, the female reaches the final phase of her sexual development, in which she is inclined to enjoy sexual intercourse with males. However, she also continues to experience the erotic tendencies that emerged in previous phases. In some females, these tendencies are constantly present with the highest intensity, while in others, they are weak and only lead to the need for sexual activity in certain conditions. Nonetheless, these tendencies exist in all females and remain throughout their entire lives.

One powerful inclination is towards incest. There is always a sexual aspect to maternal love. Just observe the pleasure with which women caress their babies, hold them close to their breasts, and touch and tickle their genital organs, even if they are barely developed. All women exhibit vaguely and unconsciously erotic emotions towards their children, and in many cases, such emotions are stronger and more developed, leading them to have sexual relationships with their pubescent sons if they followed their instincts instead of suppressing them with horror when they finally realize the incestuous nature of their tenderness.

Moreover, from the first moments of a baby's life, it provides sexual pleasure to its mother by sucking on her breasts, which are centers of sensitivity. In turn, the baby satisfies its own libido by rubbing its lips against the nipple, which is also a center of sensitivity. The first relationships that are established between the newly separated personalities of the mother and son imply pleasure for both of them. Therefore, this sensation that has characterized their early relationship remains in both of them, is fixed in their senses and soul, and is idealized and romanticized by their emotions, sung as a virtue, but it remains, in its hidden essence, in the recesses of the subconscious, as an impulse towards simple and pure copulation between the mother and her offspring. This copulation is completed naturally with other heterosexual and homosexual copulations that the mother and son have with individuals of different blood.

A young, pretty maid who, twenty years ago, served my aunt and sometimes secretly kept me company confided in me one evening that she had left the lover she had been living with for a long time. I asked her the reason for the breakup, but she hesitated and replied that she couldn't "tolerate certain filth," and so, she left. I insisted on knowing what the filth was and told her that as an anarchist, unscrupulous, and object of disapproval from my family and society, I wouldn't be scandalized, and after an hour of discussion, I finally overcame her reluctance and made her talk.

So I learned that, for about a year, she had been induced to go to bed every night with her 24-year-old lover and his mother, a shapely and attractive woman who had just passed forty. The mother watched, getting excited, the intercourse of her son with the maid and then wanted her son to possess her too. And often, under the male's eyes, there were lesbian couplings between the aroused women.

"We both make my son feel pleasure," said the mother to her lover, "and that's why we have to enjoy ourselves with each other and love each other more and more to give him the maximum amount of pleasure."

The young woman appeared disgusted as she told me these things. However, I couldn't understand how her disgust had arisen just then after she had willingly adapted to that ménage a trois for a year. The explanation came a few days later, when I learned that the girl had left my aunt's service to become a kept woman with an old salami seller who had become rich during the First World War.

In Caserta, I met a family in which incest was flourishing miraculously. Husband and wife loved each other and had proven it by generating nine children, the youngest of whom were still young. However, the father had sex with his eighteen-year-old daughter and made her pregnant. The mother allowed herself to be courted by the eldest son, who was twenty-one years old. Each of the spouses knew about the other's incestuous relationship but tolerated each other, loved each other equally, and the family lived quietly and comfortably on the father's government-job salary.

However, the good neighbors suspected something. Honest people were indignant. The neighborhood was scandalized. A report was sent to the police. The police intervened, and the daughter, pressured by interrogations and threats, ended up confessing her relationship with her father. The father, deprived of his job and sentenced to four years in prison, died in jail from sorrow, knowing his loved ones reduced to the darkest poverty. The children suffered from hunger, and the women who were looking for work could not find it because they were persecuted by general hostility. However, among the good middle-class and working-class women who bitterly criticized them, who knows how many would have imitated their example if they had been able to follow their instinct and free themselves from prejudices, convictions, and the fear of prison?

And let it not be said that these are degenerations. If this were true, all of humanity would be degenerate, and always would have been, because it has always felt the impulse towards incest.

Do not say that this is abnormal, because a need that everyone more or less feels, a tendency that is pronounced or latent, is in the nature of each individual.

ENZO MARTUCCI

Do not stupidly pretend that it is necessary to condemn these "dirty things," because everything that is natural, everything that responds to instinct, serves to give us the strongest, greatest joys of life.

Female homosexuality, like male homosexuality, is immensely widespread and arises from the desire of a woman to enjoy, in addition to the pleasure provided by men, also the different pleasure offered by another woman. The sublime Sappho, who enjoyed the company of men and who, in despair at not being loved by the young Phaon, threw herself into the sea from the cliff of Leucade, also had refined fun with girls and exalted in her poetry the pleasure they gave her:

> Of Telesilla and Attis
> Their lips were sweet to me
> And of other most graceful ones
> I loved, not without guilt[24]

In Greece, Rome, the Middle Ages, modern times, in all countries and in all social classes, we find numerous known homosexuals.

We add to them those who have managed to remain unknown and those others, even more numerous, who have suppressed their lesbian impulses, fearing to be discovered and condemned by society. We will thus have an astronomical figure that will

---

24   Gian Vincenzo Imperiale (reans.) *La Faoniade: Inni Ed Odi Di Saffo* (*The Phaoniad: Hymns and Odes of Sappho*)

include actual homosexuals, that is, homosexuals in whom the tendency is developed and stimulates them to constantly mate with their own sex. We will also unite potential homosexuals, namely women in whom the tendency is latent and, only under certain conditions, can grow, reveal itself, and determine clear needs, and we will come to the conclusion that lesbianism is present in every female, alongside heterosexuality.

Queen Maria Carolina made love to her friend Emma Lyona and together with her went to the brothels of Naples to enjoy themselves in a lesbian manner with prostitutes.

A young and beautiful peasant woman whom I met in Macchiagodena when I was confined to that village was, at the same time, the lover of her brother's wife and her sister's husband. And she enjoyed herself with both, as well as with others.

A few days ago, I read in a newspaper that in Lecce, two women, Maria Bravo and Marianna Sergi, are on trial, accused of having killed Bravo's husband, who was obstructing their lesbian relationship.

The female is driven by her lascivious nature to give herself to many males and to unite with her own sex. This proves that what Bachofen maintains is not true, namely that the woman, urged by her tendencies to give herself to only one male, was the first to withdraw from promiscuity and to establish the monogamous family, of which she remained the director for a long time. It also shows that what Forel affirms about the frigidity of women, who, according to his statistics, are mostly insensitive, is not true either. If the types he studied and questioned showed themselves to be like that, it was because women are forced by an absurd morality to deny their erotic impulses and to be more ashamed of them than men. But women are naturally lustful and inclined to eroticism not only by the need to satisfy their Messalina-like ardor but also by the desire to satisfy their vanity, which is more developed than that of men and gives them immense joy when they are sought after and loved by many individuals of both sexes.

Let's put an end to the stupid romantic comedy of the angel of the domestic hearth. Females were not born for family, fidelity, virtue, or honor. They were born for promiscuity, orgies, lesbianism, and polyandry. In their veins, the most unrestrained desires and the hottest cravings rage. And if, breaking the chains, we returned her, free, to the spontaneity of instinct, we would see her naked and shameless under the kiss of the sun, invoking, with teary eyes and spread thighs, the virile embrace of Hercules and the plump lips of Sappho.

NEMO ME IMPUNE LACESSIT

The proof of the existence of the self is not given to us by thought. The Cartesian *cogito, ergo, sum* does not prove anything at all. In fact, the judgment "I think; therefore, I am" is just a thought like any other thought: it is not identical to the object to which it refers. Needless to say, thought is a quality that presupposes substance, but quality is one thing, substance another. According to logic, substance cannot be less than quality, but it is always more than it; it always has something else besides this quality. Therefore, if quality is thought, which is an activity and, as such, is, substance could be what is not or could possess, alongside what is, also what is not. Thus, one remains uncertain whether to say "I think; therefore, I am" or "I think; therefore, I am not" or "I think; therefore, I am, and I am not."

It is a pointless objection to claim that substance can be equated with non-being. Non-being is simply *what does not exist*—it is *nothingness*. And nothingness produces nothing; it cannot generate a quality that *exists*, is dynamic, and represents thought.

But here we answer, *Non-being is what is not, but what is not is already something in itself: it is non-being.* Now we can bring up the hypothesis that it is not absolute nothingness but rather the non-being of being, that is, a reality that exists in a way opposite to the reality of being and receives from the latter, by uniting with it or encountering it, the quality of thought.

The existence of the self, however, if not proven by thought, is proven by appearance. I exist because I appear to myself, albeit in a way different from my actual existence. If I did not exist, I could not appear to myself. The lack of representation would determine the lack of representation; there would only be absolute nothingness. Therefore, if the representation presents itself, it means that the representative exists, either as a being or as a non-being or as a union of being and non-being.

Therefore, I exist if I represent myself and a world that appears exterior to me but that can objectively exist outside of me or can be projected outside by me, who still remains within myself.

Therefore, the self exists. But does it exist as it appears to me?

No, because it appears to me in a way that reflects the conformation of my senses and intellect, in other words, in a way that does not reflect reality in itself. My appearance is only a sign, not a copy, of reality. The consciousness of my self is formed by my appearance. It makes me aware of a self that is not my true self. Even this true self is revealed, rarely and incompletely, in flashes, bursting forth from the subterranean and dark abysses of the subconscious and giving me the vague and confused impression that I am not what I seem to myself but rather something mysterious and different.

The true self, the real self, is found only in the unconscious, and it is there that it is necessary to seek and understand it as far as possible, that is to say, in a minimal, infinitesimal part.

Surrealism wants to delve into the darkest depths of the psyche and, returning to the surface, believes to have glimpsed a non-logical self in which the principle of non-contradiction is cancelled and being and non-being are united, confused, amalgamated.

"Surreality," writes Breton, "is a certain point of the spirit in which life and death, the real and the fantastic, the past and the future, the communicable and the incommunicable, the high and the low cease to be perceived contradictorily."

Men have never been able to do without the principle of non-contradiction, thanks to which, they know that bread is not meat and meat is not bread; that if they are big, they are not small, and if they are small, they are not big; that they do not walk on water; and that going forward or backward is not the same thing. But the surrealists hope to succeed and plunge like deep-sea divers into the abyss of the subconscious, where logic does not operate. They try to seize the secret of the true self that they will never be able to grasp, even if some vague glimmer may tenuously approximate them to reality.

Before surrealism, other irrationalist philosophies, such as existentialism, Freudism, etc., attempted, albeit with scant results that will probably remain so, to overcome phenomenal knowledge and reach the heart of the noumenon, to discover the self-in-itself.

But the precursor of them all was Fyodor Dostoevsky, the Russian giant, the hero who descended into the abyssal depths of the human spirit and, in the dark shadows that envelop the tortuous meanderings, barely glimpsed—or believed he glimpsed—an apéiron psychological, a mixture of contradictions, a strange and indefinable blend of good and evil so tightly intermingled as to merge and interpenetrate.

And this mixture is for him the true self, the one that is deep within each of us, unbeknownst to us, and lies beneath the fragile construction of the self that we know, which is not only a product of our sensory and intellectual configuration (which can only partially falsify the noumenal reality) but also, and above all, of the education we have received, the habits we have acquired, the influences of the environment and social conventions (which end up deceiving us entirely).

For example, if, as Kant maintains, space and

time do not exist in themselves but are *a priori* forms of our sensibility that we apply to the objects that experience offers us, and if quantity, quality, relation, and mode are nothing but *a priori* forms of the intellect that condition the perceived objects, then we do not really know ourselves, but we know ourselves fictitiously as existing in space, succeeding in time, and having qualities, quantities, relations, and modes.

However, in this phenomenal self, alongside the transient tendencies dictated by appearances, certain deep, constant, irreducible tendencies are also revealed that accompany us until death and can only come from the noumenal self, from reality in itself. Egoism is one of these tendencies. Hedonism is another. We are inclined to enjoy ourselves and to prefer ourselves to every other being and everything else, even outside the conditions of time, space, matter, etc. Therefore, these are essential, eternal tendencies of the self, if the self is immortal, or tendencies that only die with the destruction of the self, if it is mortal.

Social education, imposed gregarious habits of the environment, the suggestion of religious or moral condemnation, the fear of prison or poverty, and many other forces of the same kind force us to stifle, wholly or in part, such fundamental tendencies. And then a fictitious self is formed, which extends like a crust over the surface of our soul. And it is the self of which we are conscious. But underneath, the true self rumbles, ignored. When—and here I return to Dostoevsky—a violent passion upsets us or an inexorable illness leads us slowly to the grave, when life

ENZO MARTUCCI

no longer tolerates any restraint or any lie because it must defend itself, in moments when we are face to face with imminent danger and death that wants to engulf us, then the true self breaks through, shatters the crust, and shows itself, even if only for an instant. We cannot see it well—we cannot discern its forms, features, details—but in the lightning-like and indefinite vision, we catch something that allows us to lift even a single corner of the veil of mystery.

That is why Dostoevsky studied abnormal, tormented, passionate, and sick people and described them in his books, because in them, reality more easily erupts.

I am a relativist. I know that I can only know appearances. I know that phenomenal knowledge is the only possible one for humans. But I admit that, beyond this knowledge, humans—or at least certain individuals privileged by nature—can have intuitions that allow them to grasp, albeit in a minimal way, the true self, the self that is absolute or that, even if not absolute, constitutes our inner essence, which is ignored and buried in the abysses of the psyche and only emerges when tragedy urges us.

Dostoevsky was one of the few privileged individuals and went deeper than others into the well of mystery. Following his maxim "everywhere and always, I go to the utmost limit", he threw himself into unfathomable abysses to explore the unconscious, the fearful, the inconceivable. And rising from the underground, returning to the sunlight, he declared, "Man seeks only freedom at any cost."

Yes, man wants to be free. That strange mixture of contradictions, that dark and indefinable balance of passions, feelings, and opposite tendencies that is the self, feels the imperative need to satisfy its different impulses as they emerge from its bosom. It seeks to do whatever it wants and likes, now in one way, now in another. It does not worry about the consequences; it is not guided by reason, or interest, or calculation, that is, by a single principle that regulates its actions, orders them coherently, and drives them towards a goal that ensures the concrete, lasting good of the ego. Instead, it follows spontaneity, lives in the fleeting moment, satisfies the passion that predominates at this moment, and, immediately afterwards, satisfies the opposite passion that has become, in turn, victorious in the struggle between opposite inclinations. It finds its true profit in satisfying its will, its instincts, its wildest whims. And thus, it does good and evil indiscriminately. But when man does evil, he obtains, as a consequence, pain.

Dostoevsky's anarchism leads to Christianity. God, my creator, allows me to choose between good and evil, but when I choose the latter, He punishes me, and my soul is tormented by suffering. Then I am compelled to repent, to return to good, to seek peace and comfort in the bosom of Christ. In *Crime and Punishment*, the student Raskolnikov, after planning and carrying out the murder and robbery of an old moneylender, is tortured by remorse until he is overcome and goes to confess.

Likewise, in *The Brothers Karamazov*, Ivan, the

ENZO MARTUCCI

refined and cynical intellectual who has mentally prepared for the crime, is then driven by the torment of his own soul to confess his guilt to the court that is judging his brother. Therefore, crime inevitably brings punishment.

At this point, I would like to object to the thought of the giant Dostoevsky: it is possible that my true self is absolute for me but relative to another even more absolute self that may be behind it. In this case, we would have the phenomenal self, the individual self, absolute as such, and the supra-individual self, i.e., God.

Now, what is my self: an emanation of God in which all individual selves unite? In this case, God cannot punish me for anything I do because, by punishing me, He would punish Himself. In fact, as an emanation of God, I am a part of Him, consubstantial and coeternal with Him, having His feelings, will, and intelligence. Therefore, what I have felt, willed, and thought, God has also felt, willed, and thought, and what I have done, God has done together with me.

Alternatively, is my self, my spirit, a creation of divinity? In this hypothesis, God has created me with a spiritual substance similar to His own but not His own. He has given me His perfection, but not all of it, or else I would have been equal to Him, and there would have been no distinction between creature and creator. So I appear absolute as a human spirit, as a man, as the reality that God wanted to create, but relative, imperfect, and incomplete compared to

God, whom I resemble only faintly.

Now the evil that I think and do is only the consequence of my imperfection, just as good is the product of the perfection that is in me. When I choose evil, imperfection outweighs perfection; I am not free but determined because a stronger passion triumphs at that moment over the appropriate passions, and the will fails to restrain it. Therefore, if God himself created me imperfect, denying me all His perfection and granting me only a part of it, if He composed me with a union of being and non-being and allowed non-being, imperfection, to triumph and drag me into evil at certain moments, with what justice does He then punish me when I commit this evil? With what right does He inflict punishment on the effect for which He prepared the cause?

Either God created me, like Himself, absolutely perfect, and then I would never have done evil—I would have been God like Him—or He created me as He did, and in that case, He should not punish me for anything I do.

It is useless to say, *With my will, I can restrain bad feelings: I can hold back; if I don't restrain myself, it's because I don't want to.* But precisely because I am imperfect, my will cannot always be the strongest: it cannot always succeed in harnessing passions; on the contrary, it often undergoes the influence of these passions and wants as passions want.

Therefore, the choice is dictated by the intensity of the opposing forces within me, and the stronger impulse drags me with it. My freedom consists of following that impulse and enjoying it to the fullest. If God denies me this freedom, if He punishes me when I do evil, God is a tyrant, and I should not repent; I should not submit to the Divine Will and do only the good that pleases God. I should not follow this teaching of Dostoevsky, but rebel against the Despot, deriving from it, even among infinite torments that He will inflict on me out of revenge, the supreme satisfaction of not having bent, of having defended my freedom, of having preserved my independence.

Furthermore, it could also be that there is neither the transcendent god of Christians nor the immanent god of pantheists but only matter governed by mechanical laws, as materialists claim. In this case, an unconscious universal mechanism would determine all my actions, good and bad, and there would be no punishment or reward. The noumenon, which we barely perceive behind the phenomenal knowledge and phenomenally distinguished as the internal and external world, would identify with the unique and moving matter. Remorse would only be the product of ethical-social education and the suggestion it exerts on us. The strongest types that react to such suggestion do not feel remorse for anything they do.

Life must be lived by satisfying all instincts, beyond good and evil, and only then do we enjoy intensely; only then do we gain complete joy.

Dostoevsky, a Christian, believes in divine punishment. But Nietzsche, a pagan and atheist, denies it and sings the song of beauty and strength.

Good and evil, as objective and eternal principles, do not exist. We cannot find them anywhere. We cannot find them in the phenomenal reality. If we observe it in the external world, we see that in the apparent nature, all vital manifestations are equivalent because they are all necessary for nature itself. If we study it in the human soul, we notice that all the feelings it possesses are indispensable, and what hurts us in one moment brings us good in another. Therefore, in the phenomenal reality—external and internal—there is no qualitative hierarchy among the different expressions of life.

We cannot even understand good and evil in the absolute that we perceive behind the world of phenomena. In fact, if we conceive such an absolute as infinite and eternal matter endowed with mechanical movements, then all movements are equally necessary for matter and, therefore, have the same value for it.

If we suppose the absolute to be the immanent god of pantheists, then all thoughts and actions, no matter how opposite they may seem, are necessary and determined by this god. This god moves everything from within to develop a greater harmony, and all actions contribute to achieving its end. Therefore, the Demiurge cannot praise one part of its work and consider it superior while condemning another part as inferior, because the work is equally important in all its parts. If one part were missing, it would no longer be that work.

If, finally, we imagine the absolute as the transcendent god of Christians, this god cannot regard imperfection as evil or perfection as good. To God, the existence of imperfection is just as necessary as the existence of perfection. If imperfection did not exist, if everything were perfect, the world and humans would identify with God, and God would become indistinguishable from Its creation. Therefore, both perfection and imperfection equally condition the reality of the Creator, who wants to remain distinct from Its creation. Therefore, perfection and imperfection are equally necessary for God, even though It punishes human imperfection.

Human thought cannot find good and evil in either the world of appearances or in the absolute, which it seeks to make intelligible. In such an absolute, good and evil could exist in an unintelligible way, but since we would never know this way, it would be as if it did not exist. Therefore, all that remains for thought is to reduce to pure subjectivism the principles to which it had previously attributed objectivity, to think that good and evil do not exist in themselves, that there is only my good and my evil: what pleases me and is useful to me at this moment and may not please me or be useful to me later and what I do not like and is not useful to me at present but may please me and be useful in the future.

Dostoevsky, however, does not accept this amoral conception and remains anchored to the Christian fable. But despite this, he continues to consider freedom as the fundamental requirement of man. Even if it drags us towards sin, even if it leads us to incur God's punishment, we want freedom, want to do things our way, go from good to evil and vice versa, tend "towards the ideal of Sodom and the ideal of the Madonna, which are both in our soul".

Freedom is the expansion of life. Whoever suppresses freedom suffocates life. Dostoevsky, therefore, rebels against those who, in the name of universal happiness, try to transform man into a slave and the world into a prison.

In *The Possessed*, he condemns the nihilist movement that, through a dense network of crimes, linked the conspirators together. He predicts that these fanatics, if they manage to seize power, will become fierce tyrants and cruelly oppress men to make them all equal, all docile, all obedient, satisfied sheep of the universal flock. He prophetically foresees what Bolshevism has then achieved in Russia and, by reading the papers of the Netchaiev trial, learns to know the ruthless soul that lives on today in Stalin.

But there is another, more ancient enemy of freedom that the heretical Christian Dostoevsky detests: Catholicism. In *The Brothers Karamazov*, the great thinker clearly poses the terms of the issue. In the chapter entitled "The Grand Inquisitor," he imagines that Ivan Karamazov, the hypocritical and subtle intellectual, tells his younger brother, Alyosha, the plot of his poem.

The action takes place in Seville, Spain, during the most terrible times of the Inquisition. Christ returns to Earth precisely where the heretics' pyres burn, and the people recognize him and acclaim him. But the Grand Inquisitor, as soon as he sees Jesus, has him arrested, and that same night, having gone to see him in prison, he delivers this speech to him in summary:

What was the use of suffering so much to give men freedom? You refused the temptations of the Devil to turn stones into bread, to throw yourself from the highest pinnacle of the temple and fall unharmed, to take up Caesar's sword, because you wanted the people to be free to love you for yourself and not for your miracles. But don't you know that as soon as man obtains freedom, he has no other concern than to prostrate himself, to worship someone who promises him not heavenly bread but earthly bread to sustain him?

You, in the name of freedom, did not want to perform miracles, but man cannot live without miracles and will create his own and will prostrate himself before a magician, a witch, even if he is a hundred times rebellious, heretical, and atheist. So we have corrected your work, full of heroism, and we have founded it on mystery, on miracle, and on authority. If you had acted differently, accepting the advice of the Evil One, man would have found a being worthy to entrust his conscience to and, in the end, a way to unite everyone in an unquestionably common and concordant ant hill. For in all times, humanity has always tended towards universal organization. But you did not want to, always in homage to your free banner.

We, on the other hand, will persuade humanity that it will truly become free only when it renounces its freedom and submits to us. Yes, we will force it to work, but in its free time, we will organize its life like a child's game, with innocent songs, choruses, and dances. We will judge everything, even the the most tormenting secrets of men's consciences, and they will submit to our judgment with pleasure because it will take away from them so many worries and all the tortures that personal and free decision-making costs. For having given freedom to men, you have deserved the stake more than anyone else. Tomorrow, you will be burned. Dixi.

In my opinion, Dostoevsky is right to protest against the ant hill that Catholics want to create in the name of the church and Bolsheviks in the name of the state, but he is wrong when he sees in Christ the champion of human freedom because if Christ did not obligate us to do good with the threat of stakes and prisons, as Catholics and Bolsheviks did, if he left us free to choose between good and evil and recognized our right to love him or not love him as we pleased, he confirmed that those who do good will be rewarded, and those who do evil will be punished, and those who love him and put his teachings into practice will go to Heaven after death, while those who do not love him and do not follow his morality will end up in Hell.

But here, I wonder, *What kind of freedom is it that Jesus recognizes for us?*

The choice is not free, as it is weighed down by the fear of punishment and the allure of reward. I cannot choose as I want, as I please, because I know that if the choice were to fall spontaneously on evil, I would be fiercely tortured, whereas if it falls on good, I will receive a rich reward later on. And so I choose good, even if I prefer evil.

I am in the position of a man locked in a cell that has two doors: the first, on the right, leads to a garden; the other, on the left, leads to a dung heap. The jailer comes and says to the prisoner, "You are free. Choose the door through which you want to leave. But I warn you that if you go out through the door on the right, you will find a colleague of mine who will break your kidneys with blows; if you go out through the door on the left, you will meet another colleague who will give you a bag full of gold coins."

The prisoner would have wanted to go to the right, to breathe in the scent of the flowers in the garden, but the fear of beatings and the greed for money push him, instead, to leave through the left door and endure the nauseating stench of the dung heap.

Someone may object, *It is possible for me to choose evil, even knowing that I will be punished, because the future pain is compensated by the immediate joy I get from doing as I please, satisfying my passions.* But the objection is vain: there is no compensation between a transitory joy and an eternal pain. Only exceptional men can consciously prefer the Dionysian intensity of *carpe diem* to the perpetuity of suffering. But ordinary men tremble at the threat of the flames of Hell. If they do evil, it is because they doubt the afterlife, the punishment, and the reward. Or perhaps, even believing in them, they are irresistibly dragged by their nature to satisfy their instincts, to follow the contrary impulses that emanate from their souls. But if men absolutely believed in the words of Christ and could always, with their will, restrain their natural impetuosity, they would all become saints not by free choice but by determination of greed and fear.

Therefore, Christ, by forcing us with the lure of punishment and reward to always choose good and renounce evil, stifles the spontaneity that drives us, as Dostoevsky himself acknowledges, to live freely, to satisfy all passions, to switch from evil to good and from good to evil. Furthermore, Jesus obliges us to accept and respect the law that punishes the wicked and compensates the just, forcing us to bow before the Legislator, His father, God. This is the authority that arises from Christianity.

God is the creator. God is the master. God can do whatever He wants with me. He can torture me in the depths of Hell if I act as I please. He allows me to delight in the gardens of Paradise if I act as He pleases. I must worship Him, serve Him, obey Him, accept with joy whatever He does to me, prostrate myself at His feet. But then, I am no longer free; I am a slave. And Christ accepts this slavery. Christ declares,

"I have not come to abolish but to fulfill the ancient law." Christ does not rebel against the injustice that Jehovah has committed by condemning Adam and his descendants to eternal pain but, as a good son, remains obedient to his father and, as Ferrari observes,

imagines that he can placate and satisfy him by becoming a slave to him, even to the point of suffering the extreme punishment. The father accepts the offering, has him crucified by the chosen people, then he punishes the same people for having committed the desired patricide. And this is the pledge of the new era: the ancient curse must cease because Jehovah has gone beyond his own injustice by punishing the innocent son as if he were one of Adam's innocent children. The curse ceases, but only for the chosen ones; it ceases, but justice is a mere favor; it ceases, but the freedom of the chosen ones is ordered in the void of the heavens; it ceases, but the chosen one lives in martyrdom on Earth, living as an enemy of himself, an imitator of Christ's suffering, an executioner of every instinct, and if, for a moment, he remembers that he is human, lost forever, he becomes a victim of Jehovah and Christ, united in their fury and vengeance. Christ abandons the cause of the oppressed in the very act of defending it: he leaves the Earth to Caesar, to conquerors, to barbarians; he offers nothing to the poor but the mockery of the Eucharistic bread; he sanctifies them but leaves them hungry at the doors of palaces; he gives them to drink his own blood shed by the father but must let their blood be shed by every tyrant. If he is light, his light rises to illuminate the injustice of the earth without removing it, without altering it...

Therefore, I believe that Dostoevsky should not use the mystical figure of Christ as a symbol of freedom. Jesus is not the antithesis of the Grand Inquisitor. He is the one who made it possible. If Christianity had not been born, it could not have degenerated into Catholicism, for which humanity is afflicted by a tyranny that, starting from Jehovah, through Christ, ends in Torquemada.

The symbol of human freedom, on the other hand, is another mythical character: Capanéo. The hero lying on the deserted moor under the rain of fire, the rebel who, not tamed by torture, challenges God eternally.

And it is the symbol that men should recognize to avoid ending up in the anthill that Dostoevsky abhorred.

Nietzsche maintains that life belongs to the strongest. He is right. But in order not to be killed or subjugated by the strongest, I must acquire, using any means, the power that I lack and that will allow me to resist him. If I manage to obtain it, I will stop him with my defense, and we will balance each other. Otherwise, I will fall with the satisfaction of having tried, of not resigning myself: I will die with my weapon in hand, spitting the last spurt of blood on

ENZO MARTUCCI

the enemy's face.

I will die like Bonnot, overwhelmed by the police. Or, like Capanéo, I will stoically endure the endless pain, teaching men that freedom will never belong to the one who embraces the renunciation of fools and the surrender of cowards but only to the bold, who will know how to conquer it by fighting and suffering for it, launching the supreme warning to the universe, "*Nemo me impune lacessit*."

ME AND MARIANI

The writer Mario Mariani had an exchange of letters with me in which the original diversity that separates his libertarian socialist conception from my individualist anarchist one was expressed.

Both he and I are opposed to bourgeois society and to the one that would impose Stalin on us. However, we have a different way of understanding the past and present, man and the world, history and life.

Referring to the origins, Mariani initially affirmed that our distant ancestor from whom the species began was a brutish cannibal, an antisocial animal that lived secluded with his females without seeking relations with his own kind, against whom he attacked every time he could. However, some exceptional men, endowed with greater intelligence and better feelings, managed to teach sociability to others and to bend them to mutual support, active collaboration, and mutual respect. Thus, ethics began society.

To this theory, I replied by observing that from the beginning, man possessed, alongside opposite inclinations, also a spontaneous tendency to understand and cooperate with other men. This tendency was perhaps innate and inherited from the anthropoids, if it is true, as Kropotkin asserts, that we descend from the sociable chimpanzee and not from the solitary gorilla. Or perhaps this tendency was acquired during the glacial period, when man, no longer finding the vegetables on which he fed in the frozen nature, had to adapt to eating meat and, overcoming his distinctive unsociability, to harmonize with his peers to obtain, with their combined forces, a more abundant hunt and to more easily overcome the resistance of other animal species.

Whatever the cause may have been, this impulse towards mutual aid has been evident since ancient times and has led to the birth of the first societies, within which, much later, some exceptional individuals taught others the first ethical and juridical norms to develop and better cement instinctual sociability and give union greater stability and consistency. But if the natural inclination towards agreement had not existed and had not brought men together, no one could have taught anything to their fellows because if I had the bad idea of approaching another, they would have either fled or killed me with a blow from a club, sensing danger in my proximity. Furthermore, language, which emerged as a result of relations among men, would not have existed, and, thus, I could not have communicated my ideas to anyone, even if I had found someone willing to not shun me. Therefore, sociability is, at its origins, a product of nature, not of reason.

To my demonstration, Mariani replied,

I distinguish precisely between unconscious animal collaboration and conscious human collaboration. The instinctual collaboration of swallows, bees, and penguins is, for me, an animal phenomenon that I do not call sociability. Until the *pithecanthropus*, there was also a form of animal collaboration among the first anthropoids and nothing else. Man became the king of creation when his collaboration began to become a progressive norm. You believe it was inherent in everyone, like cooking without fire because matches hadn't been invented.

I prefer to believe that some, more gifted in intelligence and emotion, have taught it to others. I do not deny that many may have had a penchant for collaboration, but I believe that some had it more than others.

Very well. However, Mariani contradicts himself. Because if it is true that "even in the earliest anthropoids, up until the pithecanthropi, there existed a form of animal collaboration", then it is not true what Mariani affirmed before, that the man of origins was a savage, antisocial *anthropophagus*. Instinctive collaboration, if it is not sociability in the sense that Mariani understands it, is not, however, also antisociality, the repugnance to approach and understand one's own kind. And why would animal collaboration not be sociability? Etymologically, this word means a tendency towards society, mutual support, agreement. Therefore, if the inclination is determined by a natural instinct or rational consideration, by a spontaneous impulse or conscious will, the consequence is always the same: it is always the tendency that exists and leads us to constitute society.

Mariani observes,

> You tell me, how could humans accept education, morals, and legal norms if there was not already a spontaneous inclination to approach each other? But even penguins, platypuses, and kangaroos approach each other to mate, choose a den, collaborate. And why don't they form a society? Why don't they accept a social contract? Because they remain at the stage of animal collaboration, bestial, and we have progressed towards human and social collaboration? Two sociabilities, as you want to call them, are absolutely distinct for me.

To Mariani's questions, I respond by observing that in animals, sociability has remained within the limits established by nature, alongside opposing tendencies that balance it, so that the animal is, depending on the circumstances, social or antisocial and thus manages to satisfy its needs with the means suitable for each particular case. In the human species, however, some men, endowed with greater intelligence and ambition, have wanted to correct and modify nature and have therefore invented education, which aims to suppress our antisocial inclinations and develop social tendencies to the maximum, until they remain the only dominant ones in us. Therefore, animals have remained in free, temporary societies, in which the need for mutual help is the only bond that keeps individuals together, who separate as soon as they can survive on their own, in changed conditions. Instead, humans have moved from these primitive societies to ethical-juridical organization. This transition, according to Mariani, was useful. According to me, it was harmful. And that is why Mariani is an enthusiast of civilization and I am a supporter of the return, or the approximation, to nature.

I think that man, with his more alert mind, would have always been superior to beasts, even if he had not organized with his fellow beings and had not created radio, airplanes, skyscrapers, and atomic bombs. And I believe he would have been less unhappy and would have found more enjoyment in life if he did not have to suppress and torment his nature to please the totems, taboos, gods, morals, rules, and laws taught by some impostors and imposed on others by deceit and suggestion.

What are the effects of education intended to mutilate, transform, reshape our personality, stifle certain tendencies, hyper-develop others, and forcibly direct our modified self towards a goal that is foreign to us?

If education is imposed on individuals who have

weak instincts and feelings, feeble will, and unaccentuated personality, it compresses and destroys the little bit of individual, genuine, and unique that these individuals had and reduces them to equal puppets, machines and automatons that think, feel, and act as the educator establishes.

However, if education is imparted to men who have strong instincts and feelings, vigorous will, and developed personality, then it violently stifles their nature. But, by stifling it, it exacerbates it, embitters it, and makes it frenetically desirous of those pleasures that are denied. Thus, when this nature can no longer restrain itself and explodes with all the force accumulated under the yoke, it reaches paroxysms and excesses that it would never have reached if it had remained free from the beginning.

But even in this case, individuals, still influenced by the precepts of education, pretend to satisfy their instincts to serve the interests of the teachers, to realize the ideas of the teachers, and to fight their enemies.

Thus, the Levites welcomed Moses' invitation, suggested by God, and slaughtered the worshippers of the golden calf; thus, the Alexandrian mob joyfully accepted the exhortations of Saint Cyril and his monks and tore Hypatia and the Neoplatonic philosophers to pieces; thus, the Muslims ravaged Asia and Africa with fire and sword to obey the command of Muhammad, who had ordered the conversion of the infidels by force; thus, the Catholics, inflamed by the preaching of Innocent III and Dominic Guzman, followed Simon de Montfort and massacred the Albigensians, raped women, and burned the cities of the heretics; thus, the reformers attacked like beasts against the Anabaptist peasants condemned by Luther; thus, the Calvinists burned Michael Servetus alive; thus, the Nazis massacred six million Jews and unleashed world conflict for the triumph of Hitler and the racial ideal; thus, American pilots, in the name of freedom and democracy, enjoyed strafing women and children who were peacefully walking in the streets of Naples.

All these people felt no other need than to satisfy their instincts, exacerbated by the suppression of codes and ethics, education and prohibition. They felt no other necessity than to fight, kill, rape, and plunder and found it convenient to do so by fighting for the holy cause, for the triumph of good over evil. In this way, they reconciled the powerful stimulus of nature with the tranquility of conscience and the protection of society.

Moreover, even today, when honest citizens lynch a wrongdoer, when respectable ladies revile the adulteress or the loose girl, when law-abiding men and order-lovers throw a chair between the legs of the fleeing thief and hand him over to the police, are they not obeying the tendency that drives them to harm their fellow men, that they can satisfy only on that occasion, while remaining in agreement with the law and with morality, and receiving a certificate of praise?

There are, it is true, individuals who act without

hypocrisy and immediately satisfy themselves without waiting for the moment in which they could do so in the service of a good cause. But society calls these individuals delinquents, brands them with the mark of infamy, and throws them into jail. And yet, it is society, in the majority of cases, that has led them to that action, suppressing their nature, exacerbating their instincts, and forcing them to explode with extraordinary violence.

These are the beneficial effects of the education that Mariani praises. He will say that this education is evil, that he too condemns it, but he wants a better, more rational, and humane education. But I will answer him that all pedagogical systems are equivalent because they all aim to suffocate, mutilate, transform nature, to shorten or stretch it on the bed of Procrustes, from which monsters or automatons emerge.

Instead, let us allow man to be himself, to develop according to his spontaneous inclinations. Let us allow him to learn on his own, through his own experience, in the widest freedom, what is useful and what is harmful to him. Let us advise him when we believe we are warning him against danger, but let us recognize his faculty to accept or reject advice. Let us make him, in short, master of himself, arbiter of his thoughts and actions.

Only in this way will it be possible to create a new humanity that is free and sincere, otherwise we will have only Jesuits and puppets.

Mariani says, "You want to reject man to the

state of nature. To remake a biological thief and murderer, free and aggressive."

Actually, in nature, there is not only a tendency to steal and kill but also an inclination to help and collaborate. Kropotkin argued that the impulse for mutual support is stronger compared to other impulses, both in animals and humans. Mariani believes the opposite and cites a judgment by Hans Much:

"The plant is better organically structured than the animal and is also more innocent: the animal lives exclusively on theft and murder."

But these are exaggerations on both sides. What is certain is that Mariani, in order to preserve education, wants man to remain a civil assassin who slaughters in the name of virtue and love.

Mariani adds,

If I have to fight to bring men back to the law of the jungle, nothing good can come of it. And then, how do I fight? With what enthusiasm? As I told you, I tried to get more clarification from you than what was in your book *Beyond*, but I didn't succeed. Just as I never find them in Stirner or Nietzsche.

As long as we remain in the critical part of bourgeois, capitalist, Christian society, we all agree, but when it comes to reconstruction, everyone responds, *we'll see how it goes.*

And I tell you that, according to the experience of the past, we run the very serious risk that it will end worse.

I asked you, *Who decides?* You say, *Not the majority, not the minority, not the dictator.* So who?

"In an anarchic world, each individual decides for themselves," I reply.

Anyone else, even if more intelligent or more experienced than me, cannot know my needs and necessities as I do. Therefore, their decision can never satisfy me.

In the absence of any law and any morality, any government and any master, I will live as I please.

If I feel like isolating myself, I will do so and take care of myself, taking from the means of production that will be put in common the land and the tools I will need. If I prefer to live associated, I can come to an understanding with others, in many different and free ways. I can try all experiences and join one of those groups that will practice the system of integral communism (common ownership of the means of production and the product of labor, where each gives according to their abilities and takes from the pile according to their needs) or one of those other groups that will achieve mutualism (collective ownership of the means of production but individual possession of the fruit of labor that remains to the individual who consumes or changes it as they wish) or even some other group that will follow a different system.

From any association, I can leave whenever I want, and, to do so, I will not have to wait for the permission of the associates as Armand demands. Because if, voluntarily, at any moment, I desire to participate in a union to satisfy a spiritual or material need, I can at another time, when this need is satisfied, leave the association, and no one can demand that I remain bound to my will of the previous day. Experience, however, will teach me that I should not be overly fickle and break every contract immediately after concluding it, otherwise, I will offer no guarantees to others, and, in the end, I will find no one willing to associate with me.

In cases of struggle, I will defend myself alone if I feel such ability, or I will ask for the help of friends, or I will establish with my collaborators an agreement by which we will commit ourselves to defend each other for as long as we remain united.

Mariani believes that the strongest will always succeed and impose their laws on others, giving rise to a new social order governed by authority. But I answer that the strongest is never so strong as to be able to remain so always, and the weaker can always seek means to resist them and balance themselves by either allying with others or resorting to cunning or devising a different strategy. Therefore, the strongest, encountering resistance, will be forced to stop if they do not want to lose their life. Command, government, tyranny will become impossible when no one is willing to tolerate them anymore. And since in an anarchic environment, individualistic feelings, the love of freedom, and the impatience of every chain would be awakened in the heart of every person,

ENZO MARTUCCI

ready to challenge death rather than give up their independence, authority could not be reborn.

Mariani also believes that a polymorphic, decentralized, disorganized society—in which there would be many anarchist groups practicing different systems, and in which each individual could, at his or her own discretion, move from one group to another or remain isolated—would not be compatible with the current civilization, with the civilization of machinery and the standards that he wants to preserve.

On this point, we completely agree: anarchy, in its universal realization, can only produce a natural life or a civilization, physiocratic and artistic, close to nature.

Today's civilization, which transforms the individual into a cog that mechanically fits into the social machine, necessarily requires a center, a direction, a discipline that conforms the activity of individuals for its preservation. Otherwise, it disappears.

But it is precisely the death of this civilization that I desire and believe is closer than one might think. In fact, if it will not be the anarchist revolution, if it will not be Stirner's crime to sweep it away, the atomic bomb will provide for its destruction. And even Mariani foresees this.

Furthermore, even if anarchy could never establish itself as a general way of life, it would still remain a reality that manifests itself in the revolt of a few exceptional and refractory individuals, of a few anomalies, strange and heroic, who, in every time and in every place, rise up against the shepherds and the sheep and prevent the absolute triumph of the herd.

Bonnot is a fact that Mariani cannot deny. The destructive power of the iconoclast is a scourge feared by supporters of order. Therefore, anarchy is far from unattainable, even if destined to always reveal itself in the form of Prometheus, who challenges Jupiter and dares the impossible.

In his latest book, *The Last Men*, Mariani indicates the best means, according to him, to regenerate humanity.

The Third, inevitable, World War will destroy our species. Peoples will annihilate each other with atomic bombs and cosmic rays, with toxic gases and scientific weapons, to serve the interests and ambitions of Stalin and his clique or of Truman and American capitalism.

Before the war breaks out, two regenerators (in Mariani's book, they are named Magda Ziska and Harry Hogarth) will take refuge in the heart of Africa or on an island in Oceania, in a wild and unknown place that will escape the devastations of war due to its remoteness from civilized life. They will bring with them many children of both sexes and educate them with a severe, draconian, and ferocious pedagogy that aims to transform the nature of the educated, stifling in them the instincts that drive them to fight, compete, and oppress and strengthening the opposite instincts that spur love, tolerance, and mutual support. They must "subject them to the pressure of a frightful moral grinder, to see if it will be possible to squeeze from their veins selfishness, cruelty, lying, perfidy, and all the vices and faults of the species and let survive, after the universal slaughter, only these few purified champions."

If any child proves refractory, if they resist transformative education, retaining all the instincts received from nature, then the educators must suppress them. They will also take care to destroy, thanks to their airplane and perfect machine guns, the last remnants of "camiti," that is, old men who have by chance survived the scourge of war. Thus, in the world, only the children educated by Magda and Harry's system will remain, who will begin a new humanity of a particular type, that is, of the type of the "angel-man," who will have "the body of Apollo Sauroctonos and the soul of St. Francis of Assisi."

So far Mariani. However, his book reminds me of an old proverb that is still relevant: the worst enemies of humanity are actually humanitarians. All those who want to correct, improve, elevate human nature create only one type of person, free of the flaws reproached to contemporary individuals, end up massacring—or desiring to massacre—all those others who are not reducible to the type they dream of.

But this is priestly fanaticism: the truth is mine, the model is in my possession, and anyone who does not conform to that model constitutes a degeneration that must be suppressed!

In such fanaticism, the inquisitors of the Middle Ages, even those in good faith like Torquemada and Borromeo, participated. They wanted to create the true type of man, the type of Catholic man who, according to their views, achieved the goal to which the species tends and for which it was created by God. Therefore, they burned alive all the deviators, the heretics, the unbelievers, the heterodox, that is, all those who, in their life, with thought or action, moved away from that goal.

Hitler also had such an aberration. He yearned to create the single type of superior man, the Germanic man, and, to achieve it, eliminated all different elements. He began by exterminating six million Jews, who, because of the Semitic blood coursing through their veins, could never acquire those characters of strength, heroism, ruthless energy, and genius creation that, according to racism, are unique to the Aryan race of which the Germans claim to be the sole heirs. Then he—inspired by Providence, which he continually invoked in his speeches—unleashed the Second World War in order to subjugate and progressively eliminate all other races considered inferior to the Teutonic one. The result was tens of millions of deaths, tens of millions of mutilated and disabled, and the world plunged into poverty and terror. Hitler, to create a superior being, plunged real humanity into the abyss.

Another priest—crazy and fanatical—of the same kind is Stalin. For him, the type of man we must reach is the collective man, that is, the conformist and disciplined man of the perfect barracks. This is the ultimate goal of evolution, the result of the dialectic of Marxist materialism. To achieve this goal, he eliminates—with inhuman ferocity and accelerating

ENZO MARTUCCI

the pace of the process of history—all those who are irreducible to the ideal he cherishes.

The great purges, the millions massacred, the Russian people reduced to the condition of serfs, the masses forced into forced labor and starvation wages under the ridiculous label of socialism can find no other origin for their misfortunes than the obsession of a maniac who believing to have discovered paradise for humanity, forces it, with kicks, to enter such paradise and cruelly crushes all those who refuse or who, once past the threshold, cannot adapt to the new Edenic environment, regulated and directed by the caporali and delighted by the police harassment, the hospital gallows, and the scurvy of Siberian exile.

Fortunately, Mariani is not afflicted with the madness of these grim priests. He does not have the soul of a Hitler or a Stalin. He is a fine writer, possesses the exquisite sensitivity of an artist, and would never be capable of machine-gunning, solely as a result of reasoning, the wretched survivors of atomic war or rebellious children to his education.

These things, in the book, he has Magda do. But he, the author of *The Madonna of the Seven Sorrows*, would be the first to oppose it if Magda were alive and attempted to carry out her fierce intentions. But here, I am not arguing with Mariani about what he is. I am arguing with the attitude of dubious taste that Mariani assumes in *The Last Men*. That is, with the attitude of Torquemada, Calvin, Hitler, Stalin, and the purifier of the species for the triumph of the new, identical, and absolute type of man.

And I say, *You are fighting for a lie. You are striving for the impossible. You will not be able to create the man-angel, just as Stalin could not create the collective man, Hitler could not produce the Germanic man, and the inquisitors could not generate the Catholic man.* There will never be a single type of man of which all others will be identical copies, even if educators and regenerators exterminate millions or tens of millions of individuals who deviate from this type.

The inquisitors burned countless heretics alive, but the detachment, through thought and action, from the church creed remained alive in many men, who did not allow themselves to be absorbed by Catholicism and the masses that were fanaticized by it. Hitler murdered millions of Jews and unleashed conquering war, but he was ultimately overwhelmed and could not inaugurate the era of the Aryan man in the world. Stalin oppresses the Russians and has accustomed them to the life of the ant colony. The collective man will never come because mammals are not like certain insects and cannot be reduced to the identity of impersonal functions. Mariani will not produce the angel, and very few of Magda's students will allow themselves to be stripped of their own characters to make themselves similar to their comrades in altruism and generosity.

And this is for a very simple reason: because a uniform humanity, all good or all bad, can never exist. It can never exist precisely because individuals are different from each other; they have generous and perverse instincts differently developed in each one,

ENZO MARTUCCI

and, therefore, each one represents a personality, a microcosm, a reality in itself, with particular needs, feelings, and inclinations that are irreducible to a collective unity in which all human beings would identify themselves.

Roscellino was perhaps not wrong when he stated that the individual alone is real and the gender is nothing but a word, *flatus vocis*,[25] and it cannot exist, otherwise, in every man, there would be two men, that is, the man and another man. In essence, if the gender is unprovable, if it is logically impossible, it reveals itself to us as a natural fact determined by physical and psychological similarities among certain individuals. But alongside similarities, differences appear, that is, what is peculiar, what is proper in each one, and that distinguishes one self from another.

If you want to destroy these peculiarities, if you want to reduce men to many identical puppets, faithful copies of a single model, then you annihilate the individual, and by annihilating it, you also destroy the species, that is, the similarities that the individual has with others from whom it distinguishes itself by its own personality. This is why a single type of humanity has never existed, nor will it ever exist.

Men will remain different, all with good and evil within themselves, all with Abel and Cain in their own blood and soul, but differently developed in each and, therefore, producing original needs,

---

25   *Flatus vocis* (Latin: "breath of the voice") is a nominalist term suggesting that universals exist only as words, without independent reality. (Ed.)

tastes, and aspirations in each individual. And even if, speaking hypothetically, Mariani could perform the miracle and generate the angel-man, would this be progress? Would it be an improvement?

I say no. Because the angel-man would be a eunuch. Nietzsche observed that passions defined as bad and antisocial are necessary for life, something that must exist deeply, essentially, in its economy. Selfishness, greed, pride, perfidy, the spirit of aggression, and rebellion awaken strength, masculinity, determination, boldness in man. Take these feelings away from him, leaving him only with love, pity, sociability, altruism, and the result will be a weak, feeble, timid, sugary being, that is, the bleating sheep, Mariani's angel.

Likewise, if you take away all the good feelings from man and leave him only with the bad ones, you will have Hitler's Germanic man, the tormentor of Buchenwald and Mauthausen, a hideous monster, a tiger drunk with blood.

Mutilated nature degenerates. Therefore, we must accept it as it is, without exclusions or limitations, with all the instincts it gives us, with the good and the bad that are both necessary. But to follow spontaneity, to live naturally, and to follow opposing tendencies, we must free ourselves from education, morality, and the gregarious habits that society has instilled in us and propose as an end not an impossible single type of humanity but the preservation of diversity among individuals that nature has created differently.

ENZO MARTUCCI

Only then will a balance be established among people, albeit a mutable and oscillating one, when each person remains true to themselves and can, with their own unique means, understand or defend themselves against others' attacks, depending on the various circumstances.

Mariani aspires, therefore, to an Edenic anarchy realized by angelic humans, who will be made so by Magda Ziska's educational system. I, on the other hand, tend towards a polymorphic anarchy lived by natural humans, who will have broken all ethical, religious, and legal constraints, following the great example of Giulio Bonnot. The two concepts are separated by an abyss, and it is possible to say that our anarchies negate each other, mutually excluding each other.

However, despite this, I esteem Mario Mariani because he is a brave writer and a sincere and audacious man who has been able to fight for his ideas and face the attacks and persecutions of fascists without ever backing down. Therefore, I deeply deplore the unfair attack that the newspaper *Umanità Nova* has launched against him by reproducing an article written 25 years ago by Camillo Berneri called "Bourgeois Mario Mariani."

It should be noted that Berneri was made sympathetic by his death because he fell victim to the fierce intolerance of Stalinist priests in Spain. But he, too, was a priest in life and fanatically attacked anyone who did not enter his church. He also longed for a future humanity of a single type that would follow a single code of conduct, practice a single social system, that of libertarian communism, and eliminate non-conformists, refractories, and rebels. His conventual anarchy was closer to Mariani's Edenic anarchy than to my instinctive, naturalistic, multiform anarchy. In 1920, when I was sixteen, he attacked me and Renzo Novatore, calling us "megalomaniacs, graphomaniacs, and paranoids, weak imitators of crazy philosophers and decadent poets, softened by opium, hashish, and sirens at so much per hour" in the magazine *L'Iconoclasta*, which hosted all the polemics among anarchists.

I could not respond because, in the meantime, I had been arrested. But Renzo Novatore, the strange and great artist who later fell heroically in a conflict with the police, replied for both of us and defined Camillo as "a library mouse, dogmatic and pedantic, who only knows how to learn but not create, only knows how to get by but not live, and hates those who, unlike him, are not satisfied with staying with their feet on the mediocre ground but put wings on to fly to the farthest skies and descend into the deep abysses."

Therefore, from being a mediocre man, Berneri, in his criticisms, used only the banal arguments accepted by common taste. He used them against Mariani too, accusing him of pornography.

But what does this mean? It simply means that Professor Berneri was a hypocrite in the classroom, a moralist from the sacristy, certainly not an anarchist. Pornography does not exist, and, as Mariani cleverly replied, it is nothing but "love of others," as the French say, in life. And in literature, Oscar Wilde, who ought to have known, wrote, "There are no moral or immoral books; there are well written books and badly written books."

To demonstrate that there are certain sexual tendencies in human nature that cannot be denied or suppressed as stupid moralists suggest, does it mean creating pornography? But then, I am more pornographic than Mariani because I went much further than him. And more pornographic than Mariani and me are Gide, Proust, Lawrence, Sartre, and all the greatest contemporary writers. And where do we put D'Annunzio? And Mirbeau, Gauthier, Flaubert? And the fine Petronius, author of the *Satyricon*? And Anacreon, Sappho, and all the Greek poets? From this, we can deduce that if Professor Camillo Berneri had lived and become the High Commissioner for Education in the Federation of Libertarian Communes in Italy, he would have expelled all the works of ancient, modern, and modernist literature from schools and libraries and kept only *The Betrothed* by Manzoni, the book that exalts moral sentiments, domestic virtues, and the unsurpassed holiness of the family hearth.

Berneri also accused Mariani of wanting to destroy the family. Well, what's so serious about that? Did the professor get scandalized? And why didn't he also accuse Plato, who in *The Republic* advocates free love and collective offspring?

The reality is this: Berneri was not an anarchist,

nor are his modern disciples, the libertarian communists, the editors of *Umanità Nova*, Pier Carlo Masini, Cesare Zaccaria, Carlo Doglio, and the like. These individuals define anarchy as their social ideal, which is instead a democratic non-state regime in which authority is exercised by the majority. Now anarchy is something more: it is a life in which there is no authority because no one recognizes it and no one submits to it. It is a life in which there is not a single social system, such as libertarian communism, but there are many different systems, many varied forms, produced by the variety of needs, tastes, and opinions of individuals. And all of these forms do not fossilize but evolve and transform, dissolve and reconstitute themselves as individuals perceive new needs or feel their dispositions or ideas change.

Anarchy is not an organized, disciplined society compatible with the current industrial, mechanical civilization but rather the restoration of natural freedom that does not take on a single aspect but is realized in different aspects through many different ways of association, understanding, various relationships, and balances variously produced among men without God and without masters.

Therefore, anarchy not only entails the destruction of the state but also of all those other organized groups that libertarian communists would like to preserve and which, like the state, absorb the individual and impose a discipline that he must necessarily accept. These groups—family, union, municipality, federation of municipalities, etc.—are chains that

ENZO MARTUCCI

subjugate personal freedom. The anarchist, on the other hand, only participates in the free group, the association in which he agrees with his comrades by his own will, not because others force him, and from which he withdraws when he wants, without anyone being able to hold him back.

Some, few, or many of these associations may attempt the experience of Kropotkin's communism, while other associations will attempt other experiences. Then communism, remaining free, not being organized, will not contradict the demands of anarchist life. But if communism succeeds in transforming itself, as its theorists claim, into a universally extended social organization that will impose on the individual the discipline of the *demos*, the norm of conduct established by the majority and its leaders or masters in every autonomous municipality, then it will resolve into a new tyranny that anarchism will have to fight as it has fought the others.

Instead of the unitary, authoritarian, and centralizing state of Mussolini or Stalin, there will be many small states, that is, municipalities, each organized hierarchically and bureaucratically, like the ancient state. At the head of each municipality, there will be a leader, elected by the masses, a Masini who, for the public interest and the collective good, will establish the obligation of communist practice for everyone and penalties for those who fail to comply. The municipalities will be federated and their relations coordinated by a central committee, presided over by an authoritative priest like Zaccaria. And there will be a new church, rejuvenated and purified, in which, instead of Pius XII, Ferdinando Tartaglia will preside.

However, such an organization that will overload the individual with rules, norms, morals, and duties and force him to the narrowest conformity dictated by a sheep-herder will not only present no similarity with integral anarchism, which is pure individualism, but not even with libertarian socialism conceived by Bakunin, Kropotkin, Malatesta, who believed in the possibility of voluntary adoption of a single social, ethical, and economic system and only in the most serious cases admitted the imposition of the majority on dissenters.

The libertarian-communist society will be built on the model of the F.A.I., that is, the pseudo-anarchist little party in which soldiers, obedient and disciplined, receive from their superiors the infallible rule of thought and conduct and attack anyone who rejects or criticizes it. And everything will go as before, worse than before, more hypocritically than before. Sheep and shepherds, comedy and deceit....

But here arises, spontaneous, a question: why do the FAI-ists, who are good people, not leave us individualists, for our ideal, the infamous name of anarchy? Why don't they choose another name for their organization, for example, that of the Italian Libertarian Communist Party?

Masini and Zaccaria would gain in dignity.

And they would be more respected by the marshals of the carabinieri and the country priests.

NO PRISON, NO POLICE

The modern libertarian communists conceive anarchy as a democratic and stateless regime, based on the commune, where the majority will establish the general rule of conduct.

The theorists of libertarian socialism, Bakunin, Kropotkin, Reclus, Malatesta, were more tolerant. They thought that in the future commune the economic system to follow, the ethical and social norms to respect, and the collective decisions to be made cannot be imposed by the majority but must be voluntarily accepted by all members. They believed in unanimity and idyllic life but also admitted a dissenting minority to whom the majority must recognize the right to try its experiments. Only if the minority attacks the interests of the majority with violence will the majority be forced to subdue it by force.

"Martucci will not want," Malatesta wrote in 1922, polemicizing with me on *Umanità Nuova*, "that, out of respect for the sacred rights of the individual, we should leave a ferocious murderer or child-rapist free to harm. Instead, we will consider him sick and lock him up in a hospital, where we will treat him."

I believe that, as by nature, the individual can do whatever he wants as long as he has the strength, so can others who feel harmed by his action defend themselves by any means. Defense is also natural, and a group can expel from its midst the one who harms his comrades, can send him elsewhere, or even kill him if the offense is excessively serious. But it must not deprive him of his freedom, locking him up in a prison-hospital, nor treat him if he does not want to. The pretense of curing, healing, correcting, straightening is most odious because it forces the individual to cease being who he is and wants to remain, to become what he is not and does not want to become.

Take someone like sadistic Clara from Mirbeau. Tell her that she needs to seek treatment to destroy her perverse and abnormal tendencies, which are dangerous for herself and others. Clara will respond that she doesn't want to be cured, that she intends to remain as she is, defying all danger, because the satisfaction of her erotic cravings, excited by the smell of blood and the spectacle of cruelty, gives her such an acute pleasure, such a strong emotion that she couldn't experience it anymore if she transformed into a normal woman and had to satisfy herself with the usual insipid lusts. Tell her that she is a monster who should be horrified of herself, and she will answer you, "Monsters...monsters! First of all, there are no monsters! Those you call monsters are superior forms or simply beyond your conception. Are not the gods monsters? Is not the man of genius a monster, like the tiger, the spider, like all individuals who live above social lies, in the shining and divine immorality of things? But I, too, then am a monster."

A famous murderer who killed women not to rob them but to violate them, to obtain the concordance of his pleasure spasms with the spasms of death of the other, confessed, "In those moments, it seemed to me that I was God and creating the world."

If you had approached him to propose the treatment that would have made him normal, he would have refused to accept it, realizing that in normality, he would not have found a sensation as intense as the one offered by his anomaly.

Therefore, wanting to cure these individuals by force, wanting to cure them against their will, would be like asking a tuberculosis patient to abstain from smoking and alcohol to lengthen his life. "But I don't care about dying first," the sick person will reply, "as long as I can satisfy myself in my own way now. It's better to live only one more year enjoying myself rather than ten suffering and renouncing everything."

Do you want to force those who want to be lost to save themselves? But then, they will no longer be masters of their existence. They will not be able to dispose of it as they see fit, and they will feel the good you intend to do as a harm.

If Clara from Mirbeau or the characters of Sade seek to torment you, shoot them. But leave them alone, and abandon the idea of leading them to repentance in the name of God and morality or of curing and healing them for the glory of science and humanity.

And besides, is it true that all those who commit a crime are sick, crazy, and worthy of the asylum and the shower?

If you ask Lombroso's science, it responds affirmatively. It defines crime as an atavistic return. If you ask Ferri's science, it tells you that wrongdoing is a product of the anthropological factor combined with the social factor. If you ask Nordau, he declares that even genius is degenerate.

This science is dogmatic and one-sided, tends towards easy generalizations, extends the results of observations on facts experienced and understood to unexperienced and uncomprehended facts, and derives an absolute truth, a pretentious but fictitious knowledge, that reduces the plurality of natural phenomena to a non-existent unity. Therefore, it creates a type of person who has no counterpart in reality and assures you that anyone who deviates from that type is a pathological subject candidate for the hospital.

But such a science has nothing in common with that other relative, modest, constantly evolving science that always doubts its achievements and constantly re-examines them, undoing certainties and moving forward on new paths.

"There are two parts to science," writes Berth,

one formal, abstract, systematic, dogmatic, a

ENZO MARTUCCI

kind of metaphysical cosmology very far from reality and claiming nevertheless to enclose this different and prodigiously complex reality in the unity of its abstract and simple formulas; it is simply science with a capital S, the science that pretends to deny religion by opposing solution to solution and giving a rational explanation of the world and its origins. And there are different sciences, concrete, each having its own method, suitable for its particular object. Sciences that grasp reality as closely as possible and are nothing more than reasoned techniques. Here, the pretense of unity of science is broken.[26]

Socialists, communists, and the creators of future cities, no longer able to accept the universal truth revealed by the religion they have rejected, receive from Science, which is unified and dogmatic, another universal truth, outside of which, there can be no individual well-being or social order. They feel the need to have their feet firmly planted on the solid ground of absolute certainty, and that is why Malatesta collects all the scientific responses on the origins of criminality.

But it is not true that only those who have marked abnormal tendencies, who are crazy and sick, commit

---

26   Édouard Berth: *"Anarchisme individualiste, marxisme orthodoxe, syndicalisme révolutionnaire"* (Individualist Anarchism, Orthodox Marxism, Revolutionary Syndicalism), *le Mouvement socialiste*, May 1, 1905, p. 9-10, 14.

crimes. Experience shows that even perfectly healthy and normal people commit misdeeds, and not only for economic reasons or causes determined by ignorance or prejudice. A young, good, simple, sincere man whom I met in prison was there serving a life sentence for poisoning his wife to live with his lover. An accountant who was with me in political exile on the island of Tremiti was the most normal, common, and mediocre man imaginable. The fascist police had sent him into exile because he harbored a communist brother. But he, the typical accountant, seemed the personification of the wisdom, peacefulness, and calculation of the middle class. Yet he almost ended up in jail because, surreptitiously, he corrupted little girls and committed acts of lust upon them. The money with which he silenced an angry mother saved him on that occasion. But he confessed to me that he had always been a satyr, even when he was free in Milan.

A friend of mine who died many years ago was a generous, loyal, noble, and highly intelligent young man. A fine poet, he fell in love with a woman who later abandoned him. One day, when he met her, his soul, disturbed by anger and jealousy, felt an imperious, blind, instinctive need to shoot the child she was carrying in her arms. "I felt," he said to me, "that I had to kill her son to make her suffer everything she was making me suffer. I held back with a superhuman effort of will. But one more moment, and I would have shot."

All men can commit crimes because in everyone's

soul, the most diverse instincts and opposing tendencies are gathered. In me, the generous ones are more developed, and in you, the perverse ones. However, in a special circumstance, under the stimulus of powerful material, sentimental, or intellectual interests, I can kill a man, and you can save another.

So what does the society of Malatesta do? Do they consider me crazy only because my will and reason have not had the strength to hold back the instinctive impulse? But the will and reason do not always succeed in restraining instincts! Sometimes, they can; sometimes, they cannot. And then, in certain cases, even if I can hold back, I do not because I think it is good to follow the spontaneity that urges me to commit a crime. For example, to kill the person who offended or harmed me. Am I crazy, then, because I reason in my own way and not like others who condemn revenge?

But the society of Malatesta wants me crazy at any cost and locks me up in a worse hospital-prison than the bourgeois prison. In fact, in prison, I only stay for a specified period, the time of the sentence. The jurisprudence based on the classical school considers me responsible for my actions, and after inflicting a punishment proportional to the damage I caused, it frees me and does not worry about what I will do. Instead, the jurisprudence based on the positive school judges me irresponsible, sick, and establishes that I must remain in the hospital until I am cured. That is, indefinitely, until the day the doctors decide to discharge me. And then, I will certainly become crazy from the cold showers, straitjackets, and other benevolent healing treatments. The repression of crime through the internment of criminals in the asylum would also require the establishment of a police force that should raid dangerous patients. But in this way, the authoritarian judicial-police mechanism would be revived, and there would be no more freedom.

In anarchy, there can be no prisons disguised as hospitals nor police officers disguised as nurses. The individual will provide for their own defense, either alone or in association with others, but without delegating such a task to specialists who would end up becoming masters of everyone.

Natural spontaneity, no longer exasperated by the repression of laws, morals, and education, will not lead us to the impossible paradise of brotherhood and love, but it will not produce a resurgence of murders and violence either.

If, instead, to maintain order and annihilate criminals, we create a new preventive and repressive apparatus, we will inevitably return to the society we have destroyed. That is, the society of rulers and the ruled.

ITALY IS DYING

Humanity is slowly dying, consumed by the most horrible of all diseases: herd mentality.

And this means cowardice, timidity, impoverishment of vital energy, disappearance of the spirit of independence and pride, impairment of the ability to defend and attack, loss of the aptitude for creation, free and original.

Unfortunately, people are becoming identical puppets who feel, think, and act all in the same way, that is, as the leaders establish. And such a frightening degeneration, which is at the same time an offense to nature and human interest, constitutes the result of a millennial religious, moral, and social education that has pushed individuals to obedience and conformity, depriving them of any individual character, any desire for rebellion, any impulse to do things themselves, to want something specific.

In the current era, herd mentality and conformity have been amplified and extended by new, unfortunately produced causes.

First, the hypertrophic development of machinery and the civilization created by it, which forces men to a greater organization, a tighter interdependence, a stricter discipline, without which, the synchronization of intentions and efforts that allows the functioning of that complex apparatus, which is industrial production, would not be possible. The worker is no longer the free craftsman of the Middle Ages who works in his workshop as he pleases and creates his work alone, giving it his own imprint, but he is the mechanical puppet who, with his colleagues, enters and exits the factory at the whistle of the siren, who, during the established working hours, is forced to stay in his department and mechanically perform the same mechanical gestures that his colleagues perform by making only one piece of the work of which the other pieces are made in neighboring departments, and who, as a consequence, is transformed into an automaton, not knowing and not being able to build the entire work alone.

Similarly, the isolated and autonomous farmer is absorbed by the large agricultural company, in which he can no longer cultivate the land in his own way or work or rest as he pleases but is forced to carry out his activity in those fixed hours, to follow a single cultivation method, the one imposed on everyone by the work manager, and to behave as everyone else does, sacrificing his will, his experiences, his individual views. Therefore, the same impersonal and mechanical work conforms all individuals.

Outside of work, they find the union and the party, standardized public services, the uniformity of essential consumption, collective and equal entertainment based on the same radio, the same stadium,

ENZO MARTUCCI

and the same cinema, rotogravure printing, the same cultural slogans, and many other influences that attract them and imprison them in a dense network of social relationships that pre-establishes tastes, customs, and habits for everyone and homogenizes them on the level of collective discipline.

The second cause of the increased herd mentality and the intensification of the military and prison-like characteristics of human society has been urbanization, promoted by capitalism, which seeks to draw many people into cities in order to regiment them and exploit them in its factories and businesses.

The ancient Greeks had understood that *eutaxia*, that is, good order in city life, is possible only in small associations. Beyond a certain number, the free understanding between individuals disappears, and the push towards the organization of the masses under the direction of leaders operates fatally.

The third cause must be sought in the diffusion of totalitarian ideologies (fascism, Nazism, Bolshevism), which, under the pretext of realizing perfect order and Paradise on Earth, tend towards an invasive and calculated authoritarian regulation of human life and individual needs, which, according to the leaders, should be standardized, guided, and controlled to the impossible.

Therefore, humanity is becoming more and more gregarious, while its leaders, dictators, teachers, benefactors, and liberators sharpen their wits to find even more oppressive measures to perfect the complex social machine. And man, depersonalized and reduced to a mechanical cog that meshes with the gears of this machine, will degenerate indefinitely if a sudden awakening of his dormant instincts and his nature, narcotized and compressed, does not return him to the living anarchy of the primordial and to the free and changing relationships with his fellow human beings.

The degenerative process of the human race and the systematic and progressive drowning of the vivid and distinct colors of individuality in the uniform grayness of collective life are not only observed in standardized countries like America or barracked like Russia but also in a country that, for the spirit, once undisciplined and rebellious, of its inhabitants, should have remained less affected by such an evil.

Italy is dying, consumed by gregariousness. Italians no longer have initiative, feelings, their own will, a sense of independence, a sense of personality, courage, pride, impulses of rebellion. They have become many sheep, content to be cured and shorn by the shepherd, always ready to genuflect at his feet, to believe everything he says, to zealously obey his orders, and to be killed for him when he demands it.

For the past thirty years, Italians have considered thinking a chore: there is the leader who thinks for everyone and communicates to all what they must consider good and what they must consider bad, what they must do and what they must not do, which ideas they are required to accept and which they are required to reject, the tastes they must have and the tastes they must not have. The sheep listen with their

ENZO MARTUCCI

mouths open, passively accepting everything, without taking stock, and, common and unanimous in their general servility, they believe, obey, and fight for the greater glory of the leader. Among the sheep, those who are more ambitious and aspire to advance a little above their peers follow the leader, become his flatterers, sycophants, shoe-shiners, slaves, and through bowing and servitude, humiliation and abasement, they manage to earn a fistful of money and a sergeant's stripe. Then they show themselves to be overbearing, haughty, contemptuous tyrants with their inferiors, while with their superiors, the leader, and the other bigwigs, they remain obedient, groveling, trembling, and supplicating. And they call this a sense of hierarchy.

Fascism was able to dominate Italy for twenty-three years, and would still dominate if the war had not overwhelmed it, precisely because of the sheepishness of Italians, who were made even more sheepish by the fascists. Benito Mussolini was a megalomaniac clown, yet his Camorristic poses,[27] his lofty speeches, his clenched fist and furrowed brows so impressed the peasants that they fell to their knees before him and were moved to kiss the hand that struck them. Under the regime, all Italians, except for very few, were members of the Fascist Party, obediently following the cords they received, enthusiastically cheering the ungrammatical speeches of the

---

27   The Camorra are an infamously tough criminal organization, dating back to the 17th century, involved in various illicit activities. (Ed.)

histrion from Predappio, and repeating, with conviction, "The Duce never makes a mistake."

When Mussolini asked the people for gold to conquer the empire, everyone rushed to give it to him, not only the rich but also the poor, even the young women who removed their wedding rings and willingly gave up their only valuable possession. However, I never gave in. For twenty-three years, I endured the most terrible persecution without yielding an inch. Five assaults—in the last of which, I was seriously injured—countless arrests, five years of political admonition, the loss of a substantial inheritance given to me by my aunt, poverty, slander, and an existence made impossible by the ferocity of my enemies did not bend me. I remember that throughout all those years, I always walked alone in the streets of Caserta: everyone avoided me as if I were a rabid dog; even my very few friends feared being seen by my side and avoided me; and when sensible and decent people saw me among the police who were taking me to prison, they commented, "He wants it. Why don't you give in? Why don't you do as we do? Ah, that boy is really crazy...."

The deputy police chief of Caserta, the supreme commander of the local police force, was, at that time, a certain Morice, a true type of police officer in the Peccheneda style, deceitful and hypocritical, bigoted and treacherous. He had already helped—and perhaps not gratuitously—the oblique maneuvers of my relatives, who had managed to take away the inheritance I had received from my aunt. Not content with this, he, a little out of natural malice and a little to curry favor with his superiors, continued to persecute me and had finally reduced me to the most cruel indigence. As a political warning, I could not leave Caserta. In that town, where I was known and avoided by all because I was an anti-fascist and targeted, I could not find any work, any means of earning a living. I received no help from anyone, the environment was hostile, and my family had disowned me when I was sixteen and declared myself an anarchist. I endured the most atrocious privations, skipped meals almost every day, tortured my brain uselessly to come up with any expedient that would save me from that hell. My nerves were strained to the point of spasm; my soul was tormented by agitation, anger, and the pain of being unable to react.

After incredible efforts, I finally managed to get a small job in a lawyer's office. However, he was immediately called to the police station and asked to dismiss me. Desperate, I found myself once again on the streets, hungry and tormented, without a way out, with a noose around my neck and the hotel bill to pay if I didn't want to end up on the sidewalk and be arrested by the guards for violating the warnings.

Everyone saw me suffer and laughed at me. "Why don't you give in?" someone asked me reproachfully. "Why don't you join the Fascist Party and free yourself from these troubles?"

But I didn't want to give in, and I was willing to risk everything rather than bow down to my enemies.

I reported Vice-Questor Morice to the

prosecutor at the court of Santa Maria Capua Vetere for "violating the freedom to work." I knew I wouldn't get anything out of it, but I filed the complaint anyway to provoke a scandal and publicly demonstrate that the police were forcing an Italian to die of hunger just because he was anti-fascist. After a few weeks, the prosecutor invited me to his office and said, "Dear Martucci, you are right. From the investigations conducted, it appears that they are indeed preventing you from working and earning a living. But if I were to proceed legally against an authority in favor of an anarchist, I would risk my job and end up in your situation as well, so I am forced not to pursue the matter"

All that was left for me was to shoot Morice in the head. I didn't do it, and I was wrong. But I loved a woman, and for fear of losing her, I couldn't face death or prison that I had already faced so many times. And I resumed the climb up the Calvary.

One day, Morice, in his office, staring at me with his malicious little eyes, expressed his intention to take revenge on me in Neapolitan dialect: "*Dicette u pappice vicino a noce, 'Dammi tiempo ca te spertoso.*" ("The woodworm said to the walnut, 'Give me time, and I will drill right through you.'") I promptly replied, "*Dicette u scarrafone nfaccia a u gnostro, 'Ai voglia e chiovere che cchiù niro e chello che songo nun pozzo addiventà.*" ("The cockroach said to the mirror, 'Let it pour—I couldn't be any blacker than I already am.'")

I was wrong. Morice managed to hurt me more than he had done until then. With the subtle perfidy of his police and Jesuit soul, he plotted the most monstrous setups against me, repeatedly slandered me, tried to smear me by all means, and finally sent me into exile, unable to keep me in jail for many years as he hoped.

The night I left prison in handcuffs and with the carabinieri, heading to the island, I found my young partner waiting outside. She had shared poverty, persecution, and torment with me for seven years. She had learned that they would take me away that night and had been waiting for hours, in the rain, to say goodbye. She wanted to kiss me, but the police prevented her. She cried and went back home with her clothes soaked from the angrily falling rain.

Morice died of pneumonia a few days later.

I was in exile for eight years: five on the islands of Lampedusa, Tremiti, and Ventottenne and three in the mainland municipalities of Macchiagodena and Isernia.

Especially on the islands, I suffered immensely. It was not allowed to go out of the four houses in the village, and in a narrow space and the eternal monotony of things and men, one suffocated from boredom and disgust. The vegetative existence unfolded uniformly between the large room and the village, the village and the large room. The policemen who watched over us often found a pastime in provoking us, demanding the Roman salute from us. Many bowed, but I rebelled several times. In Lampedusa, in 1934, among six or seven hundred political and common exiles, only I, Vittorio Domiziani, and

Francesco De Rubeis refused to give the Roman salute. As punishment, they kept us for ten days, with bread and water, in a horrible, dark, stinking underground room, on a foul-smelling bed full of insects.

In 1937, in Tremiti, I rebelled with others against the obligation of the Roman salute established by director Fusco. The police locked us up in a small cell that couldn't hold more than fifteen people and had only one window. And we were thirty, packed like sardines; the air was scarce; the suffocating heat of July gave us anxiety. We endured that torment for fifteen days, during which, one of us, the communist Ferrari, who was weak and sick, did not survive.

While we few suffered these spasms, the Italian people cheered their leader and sent their children to conquer Abyssinia and to bloody Spain.

How many anti-fascists have truly fought and suffered for their ideas? They were a tiny minority in confinement, in prisons, only a handful of men, and always the same ones; outside, there were forty-six million contented sheep singing "Giovinezza," adapting to slavery.

Mussolini, in his conversations with Ludwig, said, "I receive hundreds of letters every day from people who want a job, work, a subsidy, a concession, a profit. Everyone asks me for bread; no one has ever asked me for freedom."

He was right. Servants only care about picking up the crumbs that fall from the master's table. Freedom is, for them, a useless luxury. And Ferdinand II, King of the Two Sicilies, told my great-grandfather, who was his architect, "Don Domenico, to govern people, you need three Fs: *fun*, *flour*, and the *firing squad*."[28]

The Italians remained satisfied and calm under the fascist regime for over twenty years.

No one ever thought of rebelling.

I, just returned from exile, was in Naples and planned to blow up the headquarters of the Fascist Federation with a time bomb.

But I lacked the means, and since I couldn't procure them alone, I confided my plan to an anti-fascist lawyer, who agreed with me and promised great help. Through him, I met other people who also promised to help. But *Verba volant*;[29] in the end, I had neither the explosives nor the technician who was supposed to build the bomb, and only very little money.

I tried to do it myself. I found a mechanic in Caserta, Amedeo Di Capua, who agreed to manufacture the device and a professor, Enzo Bizzarri, who made his house available to us. I asked a friend who worked in an ammunition factory to get me gelatin and trinitrotoluene, but while I was waiting, I was arrested following a denunciation by someone I had confided in.

But how could I prove that it was true? Therefore, the head of the OVRA,[30] Pastore, who came from Rome to conduct the investigation, wanting to

---

28   In the original: "*festa, farina, forca*." (Ed.)
29   *Verba volant* is the first half of a Latin proverb that means "words fly away." (Ed.)
30   Organization for Vigilance and Repression of Anti-fascism, the Italian secret police.

obtain a support document that would make it possible to denounce me to the judicial authority, demanded that I sign a confession written by him and based on the information he had received.

I resisted for forty days of solitary confinement, torture, threats, flattery, promises of freedom and money, but they were not able to bend my will. I always refused to sign. Finally, the diabolical police officer forced me to give in by arresting my elderly mother and cynically declaring that if I did not sign immediately, he would put her in a cell, where she, suffering from pleurisy and fever, would be killed by the cold and discomfort.

To save my poor mother, who is the only person in my family who has always loved me and has never disowned me, I had to give in. But as soon as I was transferred to prison and interrogated by the investigating judge, I denied the confession, specifying that the signature had been extorted from me by force. So everyone else was released, and I remained in prison, the victim of a new frame-up plotted by the cop Pastore. I regained my freedom eight months later, in September 1943, just in time to fight against the Scholl gangs during the four days of Naples.

But I was forced to endure further disappointments. The Allies who conquered Italy got rid of the most well-known fascists but left power in the hands of those reactionary forces that had supported fascism during the twenty years: monarchy, church, capitalism, militarism, bureaucracy, police.

And the people?

Part of the Italian people have poured into the Christian Democratic sacristy, adoring the pope and De Gasperi and hoping for reward in the afterlife. Another part has been regimented in the Bolshevik barracks, under the leadership of the leader Togliatti, allowing themselves to be commanded and exploited by the red sergeants, accepting all the nonsense they feed them, and anxiously waiting for the earthly paradise brought on the tips of Cossack bayonets.

Both major parties, the papal and the Stalinist, are run by demagogues and showmen, by opportunists and politicians who, almost all of them, until yesterday, kept their fascist membership cards in their pockets.

It is true that there are also small parties, but they faithfully present the same characteristics as the major parties.

Intellectuals do not differ from the masses and are grouped in cliques in which they mutually incense each other, support each other, help each other to maintain the monopoly of university chairs and publishing houses, the direction of major newspapers, and honorary and remunerative positions. Until yesterday, all cliques recognized only one god: Benito Very High. Today, some praise the Vatican; others, the Kremlin. And they continue to pontificate, dominate, and make money. The free and solitary thinker, the true great one who recoils from joining a group and aspires to excel solely on his own merit, finds his path blocked by these cliques that stifle him with the most abject means. Giulio Colesanti, a deep and original philosopher, author of the essay on "Superior Morality," lives in poverty in a small town in Molise and does not even have the opportunity to publish his writings. But, thanks to the pope, Gonella is the minister of public education. And, thanks to Togliatti, Bontempelli did not become a communist senator—by a hair!

In Italy today, only the spirit of the church and clique, of the barracks and the herd, dominates. But to this heavy and suffocating spirit, to this gloomy fog that stifles the last flickers of life, I react by opposing the philosophy of spontaneity. I, who am more than ever fought against, obstructed, boycotted, vilified by governments and parties, corporals and soldiers, do not disarm, do not step back, but, after thirty years of strenuous struggle, remain in my place of battle, bold as Prometheus, resolute as Capaneo. And I say to man, or at least to that rare man who has not yet been completely poisoned by social influence and can recover and heal,

1. Be yourself. Stay as nature made you. Develop yourself according to your inclinations and instincts; unfold according to your particular way of existing. Do not try to become like others, but preserve your originality, your personal way of feeling, thinking, and acting.

2. Be free. Remember that nothing is above you, and even if someone or something were, you should rebel against its authority that would presume to command or direct you. You can

only taste the joy of living when you live as you like, when you abandon yourself to spontaneity and are not forced to behave as others demand. Therefore, become an anarchist. Get rid of the herd mentality that has been instilled in you to dominate you; conquer your freedom, and defend it, with every means, against anyone who wants to snatch it away from you.

3. Despise all parties. Stay away from all churches. Rise up against all governments. Reject all laws. Laugh at every religion and every morality. Make fun of what they call sacred and that demands submission and respect from you. Spit on conventions, considerations, and hypocrisies. Renew, like a new Antaeus, your strength in communion with nature, no longer compressed and emasculated. Drive away the leaders, priests, directors, educators, benefactors, in short, all the impostors who, under the pretext of improving you, correcting you, guiding you, saving you, aim only to make you their slave and profit from you. Become the unleashed titan that neither violence nor deception can ever bend.

If some men will accept and follow these recommendations, there will be, in Italy, a reaction against conformity and a principle of regeneration. Otherwise, Italians will die consumed by the subtle illness that lurks within them and that, destroying each one's personality, destroys life itself.

LIGHT IN THE DARKNESS

The Christian does not think. If they were to think, they would no longer be Christian because they would understand the terrifying absurdity of the dogmas that their faith imposes on them and the miserable contradictions in which they are forced to struggle.

Let's take, for example, the Eucharist. It is not, as commonly believed, a simple symbol. In this regard, the church does not compromise, and the Council of Trent launches the major excommunication against anyone who dares to deny "that the body, blood, soul, and divine existence, in a word, Christ in his entirety, are not actually present in the host and the chalice."[31]

And it adds in Canon VIII, "If anyone says that Jesus, in the Eucharist, is eaten only spiritually and not sacramentally and truly, let him be anathema."[32]

---

31   Council of Trent. *The Canons and Decrees of the Council of Trent.* (1551)
32   *Ibid.*

Therefore, the communicant effectively eats the man-god as, in the totemic feast, the Australian savage eats the animal he considers sacred. And both end up digesting the divinity they love, respect, worship, and venerate.

The stomach digests food. Therefore, it also digests the host miraculously transformed into all the flesh and blood of Christ. And after digestion, a part of Jesus' body becomes our blood; another part passes into the intestine, from where it then follows the fate of every food we eat and digest, and, therefore, it is also the fate of the host, of which, after consecration, only the appearance remains, while it has actually changed into the body and blood of the Nazarene.[33]

If Christ really existed and was God, he should damn those who, by exalting and worshiping him, reduce him to Cambronne's matter and relegate him to the temple of the black pit.

Some time ago in the parliament of the (Sacred Heart of the) Italian Republic, the very honorable Christian Democrat Monterisi thundered against the anarchist Donato Giordano, the custodian of the Canosa Cemetery, accusing him of having burned the body of a well-known fascist.

The defendant was acquitted in the investigation, for not having committed the act, by magistrates who were certainly not well disposed towards him for the ideas he professes.

---

33   *Ibid.*

Therefore, this demonstrates that the overly honorable bootlicker Monterisi has slandered an innocent person. But even if the fact had turned out to be true, the least appropriate person to be scandalized would have been one of those zealous supporters of the Catholic Church, which has burned countless numbers of them, both living and dead.

For the living, the Inquisitors took care of it. The Spanish Inquisition alone, initiated in 1209, claimed 429,067 victims according to Catholic data (Bandiera Catholica, Spanish clerical newspaper, July 29, 1883). Adding to these all the other victims burned alive by the Inquisition in other countries, we obtain the figure of millions of assassinated.

Not even repentance saved the heretics. With a wonderful application of Christian principles of love, charity, and forgiveness of offenses, the priests did not spare those who made amends for their supposed faults. An edict from 1535 by Mary of Hungary established that "in case of repentance, men are to be killed with clubs, women buried alive. If there is no repentance, men and women are to be burned alive."

Cecilia, in her *Storie segrete delle famiglie (Secret History of Royal Families)*,[34] tells how in the dungeons of the Inquisition of Madrid, the good Dominican fathers poured molten hot lead into the intimate parts of women accused of heresy.

---

34   Giovanni La Cecilia, *Storie segrete delle famiglie reali o Misteri della vita intima dei Borboni di Francia, di Spagna, di Parma, di Napoli, e della famiglia Absburgo-Lorena d'Austria e di Toscana* (1861).

And King Philip II, a sadistic and monstrous paladin of Catholic fanaticism, attended those shows, enjoying them.

The Inquisition was the product of an alliance between the church and the monarchy, an alliance that, for about five centuries, allowed ecclesiastical tribunals to judge and condemn heretics to death, who were then handed over to the secular arm for the execution of the sentence. And even today, the church, through its theologians, claims the right to restore that state of affairs.

In the work *De stabilitate et progressu dogmatis*,[35] (*On the Stability and Progress of Dogma*) approved by Pope Pius X and printed in 1910 in the Vatican's printing house, the Jesuit Lepicier wrote, "If the times were not so perverse for the church, it should denounce heretics to the civil power, and kings should exterminate them in their kingdoms under penalty of excommunication and loss of the throne."

As for the dead, it should be noted that Catholic priests have also burned them. The Crusaders of Simon de Montfort, who, accompanied and blessed by the papal legate, exterminated all the Albigensians in 1209, opened the tombs of the heretical bishops in Béziers and elsewhere and burned their corpses. But there is more. Some centuries before that, Pope Stephen II, who succeeded Pope Formosus in the chair of St. Peter, had the corpse of Formosus, who

---

35   Alexis-Henri-Marie Lépicier, *De Stabilitate et Progressu Dogmatis* (Rome: Typographia Polyglotta Vaticana, 1910)

had been his bitter enemy in life, exhumed, tried, and convicted. Then, in the presence of Stephen, the clergy, and the entire people, the executioner cut off one of the dead man's hands, soiled his face, and then burned him completely, throwing the ashes into the Tiber.

Therefore, even if the caretaker of the Canosa Cemetery had done what the very honorable Monterisi reproached him for, a zealous Catholic could not really be indignant for so little, because the anarchist Donato Giordano would have imitated, weakly, a Roman pontiff.

Man has never been as disgustingly sheep-like as he is now. He has never marched so perfectly in step, never felt a reverential fear of authority, like he does in the stupid twentieth century. Humanity has transformed into a multitude of puppets, striving to make themselves more and more alike and to think, feel, and act in one way only, as dictated by the leaders.

Just the appearance of a police uniform, and everyone begins to tremble and bow down. Thirty years ago in Naples, when a municipal guard informed the carriage drivers that, by order of the mayor, they could not stop in a certain square or other place, all the drivers, in instinctive rebellion against the law, would stop in the forbidden spot. And if the guard wanted to issue a fine, they would get down from their carriages, whips in hand, and make him flee. Today, such a spectacle of indiscipline is no longer seen; even before the officer has finished speaking, all the drivers immediately follow his orders.

The fools say that this is progress, but I add, *towards sheepishness.* Life is increasingly, meticulously ordered, regulated, uniformed, civilized, but individuals become so many identical marionettes, moving as the puppeteers pulling the strings want them to. And impostors, politicians, demagogues profit from the general herd mentality to transform themselves into revered leaders, into superior chiefs, into esteemed manipulators of the puppets who believe, obey, and allow themselves to be fooled.

Today, any Pulcinella who shouts in the square, "I have discovered the infallible recipe for universal happiness. I have found the earthly Paradise. Follow me, and I will lead you there" immediately finds a hundred thousand supporters or a million sheep who drink his nonsense, clap their hands, and let themselves be directed and commanded by him. In this way, Pulcinella forms a political party, and if he succeeds in defeating rival Pulcinellas who lead opposing parties, he becomes the head of the state and dictator. Then, as a first step, he begins to oppress, exploit, and strip the idiotic people to fill his pockets and those of the little Pulcinellas surrounding him, of the hierarchs and hierarchettes who help him deceive the masses. But the more this mass is whipped and shorn, the more it continues to bow down and shout, "The leader is great. The leader is sublime. The leader is always right." And the leader, by constantly hearing repeated that he is great, sublime, a god on Earth, by seeing everyone bowing and lavishing praises and burning incense at his feet, becomes ecstatic, hypnotized, and ends up truly believing that he is the Heavenly Father or invested with a divine mission. Consequently, he wants to change the face of the world, create the new humanity of a single type, namely the type he likes, immortalize his name, extending his dominion over the entire globe and realizing his ideal. In his soul reigns a strange mixture of selfishness and fanaticism, and his will is determined not only by the need to oppress and milk the subordinates to live his life well but also by the concern to use these subordinates as means for the creation of his masterpiece, the new universal order he wants to establish. Therefore, Hitler unleashes the war, dreaming of Germany as the mistress of the Earth and the German race that adores him as a god and dominates and eliminates inferior races. Therefore, Mussolini raves about the reconstruction of the Roman Empire and hurls Italy into chaos. Therefore, Stalin reduces two hundred million Slavs to poverty and slavery to procure the strength and wealth that will allow him to impose the Bolshevikization of the world tomorrow. But if these false great men, these odious despots, half priests and half filibusters, can trample and overwhelm humanity into the abyss, the fault is still that of the people who raise them, follow them, and let themselves be slaughtered. If there is no servant, there can be no master. Ergo, men have what they deserve.

Mussolini, Hitler, Stalin, Franco, Peron, and others are the worthy shepherds of the stupid and mangy human flock of the twentieth century.

But to destroy the herd mentality, it is not enough to simply transform the political and economic organization of society, to move from a bourgeois state to a socialist state, or even to abolish the state and replace it with a federation of autonomous municipalities, which would be a new disguised state.

To annihilate herd mentality, it is necessary to awaken in each individual the natural instinct for freedom, the intolerance of any chain, individualistic feelings, and the need for expansion. By nature, man is born anarchic. The newborn child wants to move as he pleases, stretch or fold his legs, reach out his arms, and roll over in the crib, and when the mother wraps him in swaddling clothes that paralyze the flexibility of his movements, he rebels and protests with crying. The child instinctively feels that personal freedom is the necessary condition for living intensely. But this spontaneous tendency is immediately suppressed by parents who impose on him, through education, suggestion, and punishment, not to do what he wants but only what Mommy and Daddy command.

As the child grows up, he is sent to church, where the priest teaches him to obey God and fear his wrath. Then he enters school, where the teacher tells him that he must not live for himself but to be useful to society and fulfill the duties prescribed by it. Finally, as an adult, he enters social life and is forced to conform to all the laws, rules, and conventions to avoid the penalties of prison, the torments of poverty, and the contempt and persecution of honest people. Thus, little by little, subjected to so many narcotic influences and so many suffocating coercions, man represses the natural instinct of freedom into the depths of his subconscious and acquires herd habits and needs.

But it is precisely from such habits and such needs that it is necessary to free oneself. And to succeed in this, one must convince him that he was not born to obey but to be free, that he must not stifle his natural impulses but follow them without shame, that he must not submit to any discipline or norm but do whatever he wants because nothing is forbidden or permitted but everything is allowed for those who have the strength.

If many men will be convinced of this and act accordingly, organized society will break down, all religious, ethical, and legal chains will fall, and we will have a return to nature and the triumph of the instinctive freedom of the individual. If only a few men remain convinced, these few will hinder, with thought and action, the frightening growth of gregariousness in our species and the absolute identification of man with the sheep, but they will not be able to renew the world.

Trotsky recounts in his memoirs that having asked an anarchist, his fellow inmate, how railways would function in a world without authority and without a state, he received this answer: "If they cannot function, we will do without them." Then, Trotsky adds, "I understood that it was not worth talking about it anymore, that is, that anarchy is an absurdity."

ENZO MARTUCCI

But such a judgment can only be given by those who are afflicted with the incurable myopia of the Marxists.

Freedom is a thousand times more necessary for man than all the trains, machines, airplanes, and radios. A free individual in the middle of a forest, living like a savage, feels satisfied and content in a way the miserable follower, imprisoned in civilization and forced to always do what others want and never what he wants, never does.

The Cynic philosophers rightly identified happiness with independence. Antisthenes and Diogenes taught that man must try to suffice for himself as much as possible and must satisfy only natural needs, renouncing the artificial ones that make him a slave of society. The true man they intended to realize was the man of the state of nature; family, city, political rights were convention and artifice for the Cynics, who declared that the sage is a citizen of the world.

First of all, the sophists had understood that anarchy is the only form of life for which man is born. Protagoras, by denying the existence of any universal norm, had affirmed that the individual is the measure of all things; Callide had railed against the education that takes away from children their natural vigor, renders them unfit, equalizes them all, and accustoms them to servile obedience; and Archelao had said that good and evil are not by nature but by convention, that the strongest makes the law and also establishes what is good and what is bad, that the law is made only for the man who does not have the strength or audacity to escape it—and he who has the strength can laugh at all laws—and what appears just can well prove unjust.

In the Middle Ages, the Arab philosopher Abubacher, in his novel *Hayy bin Yaqzān* (*The Awake*),[36] demonstrated the superiority of the free and unfettered life of the state of nature over the enslaved and unhappy life that man lives in civilization.

With the advent of modern times, Rabelais suggested to man, "Do what you want", and in the last century, Stirner and Nietzsche demolished all religious, moral, and social constraints that oppress the individual and incited the latter to satisfy his egoism without caring about anything else.

Therefore, in all times and in all places, great thinkers not subservient to the flock and its shepherds have provided the rational justification for that deep need that untamed men feel: to live, following their spontaneity, in the widest freedom.

If philosophers belonging to different schools have recognized in every age that the goal of man is not to submit to others but to free himself from all chains to move at his own pleasure, this means that anarchy is not an absurdity as Trotsky believed; it is the state of nature that, if restored, will offer men the joy of existence that they have lost for millennia and that they would lose even worse in the Bolshevik, Trotskyist, or Stalinist barracks.

Dear Martucci, when one talks with you, one

---

36   Ibn Tufayl: *Hayy bin Yaqzān* (Ed.)

feels like a beast. Only we cannot all become beasts again because man has become accustomed to civilization and does not know how to live outside of it.

So said to me a young and pretty painter, who, evidently, wanted to repeat in my regard the judgment that Voltaire issued about Rousseau: "When you read him, you feel the need to walk on all fours."

And it seemed to her that such a judgment was more suitable for me than for Rousseau. Because while Gian Giacomo, while maintaining the superiority of the state of nature over civilized life, believed it impossible for the entire human race to return to it and advised the latter to accept democracy as the necessary lesser evil, I instead think that our species could return or come closer to its origins. That is, it could awaken in itself dormant instincts and natural tendencies that push it towards greater freedom, reject all law, authority, and discipline—in other words, everything that represents the indispensable condition for the preservation of organized society and artificial civilization—and realize an anarchic life that would unfold through countless forms, ranging from the primitive state, pure and simple, to the semi-primitive state, up to the free civilization, adhering to nature and never separating from it, which would be produced by groups and communities of farmers, artisans, artists, and thinkers, freely associated.

But, as the painter observes, man who has

acquired gregarious habits and artificial needs would no longer be able to adapt to such a life. However, I draw her attention to a fact: man has become accustomed to the science of the flock, judges it beautiful and good, deems it necessary, cultivates the sheeplike feelings and unnatural needs that society instills in him, but in him, the instinctive need for freedom remains, suffocated and repressed, and he suffers from the impossibility of satisfying it.

Let us take, for example, the worker. He has become accustomed to entering the factory every morning at six when the siren sounds, huddled among his comrades. He has become accustomed to staying in his department for eight hours, always automatically performing the same gestures and getting tired in a job that does not excite him because it does not require the use of intelligence and creative ability but is mechanically executed. However, no matter how accustomed he is, no matter how convinced he is that that life is necessary and must continue in the same way, the worker suffers from feeling trapped in the factory without being able to leave before the scheduled time is up; he suffers when, exhausted, he cannot interrupt the work and rest for a few minutes because he is watched by the police eye of the department head; he suffers when the latter scolds him and raises his voice. This shows that instinct never fully adapts to the slave life of the industrial galley.

The soldier believes that it is his duty to serve the country and obey superiors; however, he does not like the discipline of the barracks, and the orders

ENZO MARTUCCI

often irritate him. He would like to escape and be free. In the end, he submits, but he submits with pain, overcoming his nature.

The brother who feels a sexual impulse towards his sister immediately suppresses such an impulse if he is, as the moralists say, an honest man and feels ashamed of himself. However, he suffers from the lack of satisfaction of his incestuous desire.

The hungry person who, with a greedy eye, looks through the restaurant door at the succulent foods that the gentlemen are eating instinctively tends to grab the plates and fill his empty stomach. He restrains himself, thinking he will be arrested, condemned as a thief, and covered in shame. But he suffers while restraining himself.

Therefore, in everyone, even in the most socialized individual, the tendency to satisfy one's own needs, to do as one pleases, to move as one desires is revealed. The socialized person tries to stifle it in himself, but he can never completely destroy it. He weakens it by constantly repressing it, but he can never annihilate it. On the contrary, in some people, repression exacerbates the constrained tendency.

So, if people decided not to restrain their nature anymore and follow their impulses, holding them back only when extreme necessity requires it and the strength of will allows it, then they, restored to the spontaneity for which they were born, would feel intense pleasure and would be so comfortable that they would easily give up the gregarious habits and artificial needs imposed by society to maintain slavery. And their children, born in a free environment, raised naturally like Rousseau's Emile, would be even more natural and spontaneous than their fathers. Humanity would finally regain its life.

Moreover, today's industrial and mechanical civilization is destined to disappear even if there is no anarchic awakening of the human individual, and it will have to die for the same reason that the other civilizations that preceded it have died: because they have become too detached from nature, opposed to it, and, with the pretense of improving and correcting it, they have pushed men to stifle it with their brakes and falsify it with their artifices. And nature, which, if it changes, wants to change by itself and not by the coercion of man, has taken revenge by determining men to destroy civilizations and themselves.

Some writers argue that the inhabitants of the submerged Atlantis had reached a very high degree of culture and civilization. They had managed to discover and direct a mysterious force of nature, a formidable hypnotic energy, the Vril, with which they acted not only on other men but also on material things. Thus, they performed incredible miracles, built gigantic monuments, forcing the boulders to overlap, diverted the course of rivers with their will, and more. Well, they ended up using the Vril in their internal wars and caused such cataclysms that the continent was plunged into the sea.

Now, if there is exaggeration and fantasy in all this, it is not to be excluded that Atlantis and its

ENZO MARTUCCI

inhabitants—of whom even Plato assures us that they really existed—disappeared as a result of the use of a mysterious natural force that they had discovered and extensively employed.

The ancient Egyptians had also managed to seize unknown energies, and it is said that the temples of Thebes were illuminated by a magical light similar to that of the Sun. However, wars and all kinds of scourges destroyed Egyptian civilization, which never rose again.

Currently, after having compressed nature in every way, after having disturbed its balance with all kinds of subversions, after having blindly employed certain forces of unknown origin and what effects they produce in the relationships between cosmic elements, we have reached the point of disintegrating the atom and unleashing that formidable energy that nature has concentrated in the tiniest particle of matter because, for nature, it is necessary that it remains in it. However, we have wanted to seize and use it for our purposes. But it will be this energy, imprudently unleashed and used by us, that will destroy us.

The next war that will inevitably break out—if an anarchist revolt of men against their governments, their social forms, and their tyrannical civilization will not prevent it—will be fought with the atomic bomb. And hundreds of these bombs will annihilate not only the mechanical industrial civilization, not only the immense metropolises, but also the entire human species with their terrifying destructive power.

We will probably all die. But it may also happen that a few will manage to survive. However, they will be affected by degeneration due to the effects of the rays coming from the atom's dissolution. Corrupted creatures born with fundamental bodily defects will arise, children with six fingers and girls with eight pairs of breasts,[37] as predicted by the writer Aldous Huxley in his recent novel *Ape and Essence*. The survivors, reduced to a state lower than that of animals, will no longer know how to cultivate or weave; indeed, they will no longer be able to cultivate because the land will have been consumed by erosion and sterilized by the rays. And to protect themselves from the cold, they will have to dig among the rubble and take clothes from the corpses.

Therefore, men are now faced with the dilemma: either to return to nature of which they are a part and harmonize with everything without pretending to change it, correct it, or govern it anymore or to continue to tyrannize nature and then be annihilated by its revolt and reduced to the state of inferior beasts, below snakes and toads.

Man is warned. He can choose as he wishes.

The magazine *L'Unique* in June 1949 shows, with statistical data, the terrifying increase in the human population, which is happily advancing towards the figure of three billion individuals and will eventually die of hunger because the products of the Earth will

---

37   This has already been addressed: see Testut or another human anatomy treatise. (L'Ed.)

not be enough to satisfy everyone's needs. From this bitter prediction, Armand's organ—a supporter of birth control—concludes the need to "protect nature from its own excesses."

However, I believe that the overpopulation of the globe is not due to nature's excess but to civilization, morals, and laws that humans impose on themselves.

Nature has given us the tendency to satisfy our sexuality in a way that leads to reproduction. But it has also given us the tendency to seek other forms of erotic pleasure that exclude the consequence of children.[38] The inclination towards cunnilingus in males and fellatio in females, the need for anal intercourse, which is preferred by many over common intercourse, and many other impulses that drive us towards so-called depravities come from nature and allow the satisfaction of heterosexual needs without causing procreation. And such an instinct exists in both civilized and savage men and beasts. Karsch, in his interesting work *Päderastie und Tribadie bei den Tieren* (*Pederasty and Tribady among Animals*) has shown that homosexuality is widespread among mammals, birds, fish, insects, etc. Therefore, if humans were to satisfy their different tendencies according to the

---

38   To limit births, it would be enough, as we mentioned in a previous note, to follow the "law of Hyginus" — evidently ignored by the author — which allows conception only when desired (see, on this topic, "The Eye in the Alcove", from our edition). And this without resorting to degenerative eroticism or unnatural and harmful contraceptives. (L'Ed.)

whim of the moment, if they satisfied this or that tendency at the moment when it manifests itself more strongly than the others, then they would be inclined to enjoy in various ways, and births would become less frequent.

Instead, for millennia, civilization has prescribed to man, through its morals and laws, to enjoy in a particular way, that is, in the way that causes reproduction. Many who feel the need to enjoy other forms of pleasure are forced to abstain because they are terrified of the idea of the sin they would commit, of the divine punishment that would fall on their heads, and of the contempt with which men would label them if they knew they were depraved and amoral. Others who don't care about prejudices still have to give up the forbidden pleasures for fear of legal repression and imprisonment. Therefore, except for the nonconformists who challenge society or manage to satisfy themselves in secret, the vast majority of men are obliged to vent their lust in the only permissible sexual form. And then, how can one be surprised by the impressive increase in the species, and why blame nature that, if left free, would not have produced excesses?

In the primitive state, there is no private property: the land and all the resources of nature are available to everyone, and each can use them as they see fit. In the civilized state, some men have taken possession of the land and every other means of production created by nature or human labor and said, "This is ours."

The others, that is, the vast majority of men who remain deprived of everything, must resign themselves to working as slaves for the owners who exploit them excessively, paying them meager wages. And those who are not hired by the bosses, those who remain unemployed, are condemned to slowly die of hunger. If they rebel, if they use any means to wrest from the lords the bread that the lords deny them, the state throws them in jail or kills them in the squares, and all the sheep, honest and decent people, condemn them.

Even Errico Malatesta, who declared himself an anarchist and preached the revolutionary expropriation of private property, called the individualist anarchist Jules Bonnot a "common thief and criminal." Bonnot, along with a few companions, in the years 1912 and '13, audaciously assaulted and looted several banks and jewelry stores in Paris and finally fell, with his weapon in hand, in a bloody conflict with the police who were trying to arrest him.

According to Malatesta, Bonnot's actions were to be condemned because expropriation should be collective and not individual. The former leads to a radical transformation of human society and the elimination of the evils produced by private property, while the latter leaves everything as it is and only results in the transfer of property from one individual to another.

Malatesta's argument seems to make sense, but it doesn't hold up at all. If I, as an anarchist, incite slaves to revolt and expropriate property that should be put into common ownership but these slaves, paralyzed by herd mentality, stupefied by religious and moral precepts, terrified by the law and the police, do not listen to me and accept the whip and hunger resignedly, then I cannot remain a sheep because the others want to remain sheep. I am not bound to them, I am not obliged to act as they do, but I must live for myself, in my own way. I must immediately achieve my complete liberation, which for me is more important than the liberation of humanity that kisses the hand that tortures it. So I rise up alone, and if I succeed and escape death, I have the means to live well, to not be exploited, to procure satisfaction for myself, and to fight more effectively against the society that I despise.

It is not true that everything remains the same, because there is one less slave. And the example of this slave breaking the chain also shakes those other slaves who are not yet completely resigned and encourages them to follow the illegalism of the rebel. Action has a better influence on awakening people than speeches. So if I strike private property, others will imitate me and also strike it, and it will weaken more and more while the spirit of impatience, irreverence, iconoclasm, and insurrection will develop more strongly.[39]

---

39   Theoretically, this argument seems to "hold up," but practically, no. How many followers did Bonnot have? And, if the theory supported by the author were true, the many thieves who "operate" daily, how do they change society? They may not be exploited, but they are, nonetheless, exploiters. (L'Ed.)

The anarchist expropriators will not become bourgeois after the expropriation, as Malatesta feared, but they will have better opportunities to fight against the society they hate. And even if someone becomes bourgeois, the transfer of private property from one person's hands to another will not have been useless even in this case, but it will have served to ensure that enjoyment is not always for one person and suffering is always for another and that there is at least some rotation.

The pope excommunicated the Bolsheviks to incite the hatred of fanatical Catholics against them and to give the next war against Russia the character of a crusade, in defense of the faith, for victory over the infidels. Pius XII anathematized them in the name of Christ, whom he claims to represent on Earth, and shows the soul of legitimate authority opposed to the tyranny of the red usurpers.

Stalin, for his part, tries to create national churches, subject to the state and, therefore, enemies of the Vatican and dependent on the Kremlin, in the countries he dominates. In Hungary, Poland, Czechoslovakia, etc., the followers of the fierce Georgian exalt him as the true continuator of the work of Christ, which, betrayed and abandoned by the Roman pontiffs, is today carried out by the already atheist dictator to whom, in January 1946, the Bishop of Leningrad said, "You are the incarnation of the best of Russian religious traditions: it is thanks to the Soviets that the church has achieved a spiritual prosperity that it has not seen for centuries."

Therefore, Christ is on this side of the Iron Curtain at the service of the interests of Anglo-Saxon capitalism and the theocratic dream of Pius XII; beyond the Curtain, he is an instrument for the triumph of Russian imperialism and the universal domination of the Little Father, Stalin.

But there is a serious reason why all those who want to command and become absolute masters of humanity claim to represent Christ and prosecute his work: because Christ embodies the principle of divine authority, against which, every rebellion is sacrilege; because he preaches obedience to superiors and resignation to pain and, thus, induces peoples to endure slavery and not to seek to escape the pains that the state of slavery entails; because he consoles with the promise of reward in the afterlife and provides that hope without which, men would rise up to live better on this Earth.

This is why the pope, Truman, and Stalin speak in the name of Christ and prepare, for his glory, the future slaughter.

But precisely for this reason, those who aspire not to become victims of the atomic bomb and cosmic ray, those who do not want to be slaughtered for Stalin or the Yankee capitalists but aspire, instead, to the conquest of freedom must gather around the banner of the antichrist.

This is a symbol of anti-authority, anti-state, anti-herd. Waving it slaps the impostors who govern, awakens the sleeping servants, urges the resigned to shake off their inertia and actively fight for a better life.

It exposes all the deceptions with which, for thousands of years, man has been convinced to burden himself with chains and suffocate his nature and instincts. Finally, it reveals the last Jesuitical lie that, by conferring on the imminent war the chrism of holiness and divine blessing, will drive the slaves to massacre themselves, as always, for a cause that is not theirs.

The banner of the antichrist is the sign of the resurgence. It is the banner of an impulse that could still prevent the bloody conflict and regenerate humanity in the longing for anarchy. And even if the masses, stupid and sheep-like, do not know how to recognize it and do not want to save themselves by accepting it as their own banner, it will remain—until the near day of total destruction—the flag of those few who will oppose the tragic no of a desperate revolt to the general yes of the cretinized peoples led to slaughter.

Thus, the black flag of the reprobates and outlaws, the pirate flag of Stirner and Bonnot, will be the animating force of the last heroism in the shameful gregarious world that the atomic bomb will bury.

The newspaper of the fascists,[40] *Umanità Nova* (which Mario Mariani rightfully calls "*Decrepit Humanity*"), published in its issue of October 2, 1949, a piece with a convoluted and confused style titled "Indiscipline for its own sake?"

---

40   Martucci mocks the anarchist paper. (Ed.)

Reading this article brought to mind the old Latin maxim "Sutor, ne ultra crepidam," which means, "Shoemaker, do not go beyond the shoe. Do not speak about what you cannot understand."

Indeed, the author of the article—who signs with the pseudonym Taglia—reveals the mentality, vain and pretentious, of the little teacher, well stuffed with clichés and conventional precepts, of school lies and educational presumption, that is, the mentality of the fool who puts on airs and is least suited to understand, and even less to criticize, two supreme expressions of the anarchist spirit: individualism and indiscipline.

According to Taglia, these two expressions not only gave rise to the Risorgimento, which "unfolded through individualistic episodes," but also to interventionism, D'Annunzianism, and, finally, to fascism of "I do not adore the masses," of "the hard life of the strong man," of "the hero," in other words, fascism that "on these purely individualistic-heroic themes weaves its anti-bourgeoisism, the ultimate expression of a small bourgeoisie insatiable for sensations, incurably sick with nationalism, voluntarism, the beautiful gesture, youth, war—the hygiene of the world."

Now, if it is true that fascism had, in its initial propulsion, individualistic and Nietzschean impulses (discomfort with gregarious adaptation, the need to assert oneself and prevail, the mania for struggle and attack), it is also true that fascism was able to establish itself as a dictatorship precisely because the overwhelming majority of Italians were inclined towards sheepishness, the inclination to submit to the strong, to be commanded and directed. If the Italians had had the same individualistic and Nietzschean spirit as the early fascists, if they had wanted, like them, to live intensely, not tolerate constraints, and run wild rather than bow their heads, then they would have rebelled against the fascist aggression, they would have opposed "will to life" to "will to life," truncheon to truncheon, bomb to bomb, and the establishment of Mussolini's dictatorship, or any other, would not have been possible.

Equilibrium is only formed among equals, among proud men, among individuals who, while naturally different, all know how to defend their freedom using every means. In this case, they contain each other, and no one can oppress the other, who resists and fights back rather than submitting.

But if, on the other hand, there is a group of wolves on one side and a flock of stupid and bleating sheep on the other, it is natural and inevitable that the former will devour the latter. Therefore, the victory of fascism is not due so much to the individualistic and combative spirit of the first fascists as to the lack of individualistic spirit, i.e., the herd mentality, of the Italians.

And if we want to prevent new fascist experiences from delighting us, we should not preach the Christian and sweetish morality of "respect your neighbor," "limit yourself and be virtuous," "remember that your freedom ends where that of others begins."

Ultimately, this morality only manages to put people to sleep, depriving them of every natural energy and leaving them defenseless at the mercy of those who have the wisdom to follow only their instinct.

Instead, we must tell everyone, "Be individualistic. Live your life your way. Don't let yourself be sacrificed. If your neighbor attacks you, don't submit, don't humiliate yourself, but defend yourself. Try to multiply your strength, try to acquire new ones. Die rather than renounce your freedom."

And if individuals accept and practice these tips that are reflected in their nature, freed from the suffocation of discipline and social education, no dictatorship—fascist or not—can settle in anymore, and slavery will disappear from one end of the globe to the other. However, according to Taglia, the type "who builds the world around the axis of his own person remains out of a time in which the scene is played, for the first time, with a sure step, by social masses, out of a time in which the historical turning point is towards communism (not Bolshevism), in which social and moral solutions are only in the collectivity as a sure guarantee of economic freedom and the free formation of the personality of the individual."

However, how can we achieve the free formation of the individual personality when this individual is reduced to a passive receptacle, dominated by external action, and social and moral solutions should not be sought within oneself but rather accepted from the organized collective, behaving with others not in the way that he feels and finds best but in the manner prescribed by the majority? This is a mystery that only Taglia seems to understand. To me, it seems that his anarchy does not aim to break down the current society into free, autonomous, decentralized individualities but rather wants to transform it into a new society that is more barracks-like than the current one, a homogeneous society with a single economic system, a single social structure, and a uniform discipline established by the masses that dominate and to which the individual cannot oppose but is instead forced to accept their ideals and codes of conduct. It is a revised and corrected copy of the Bolshevik Russia, which Taglia seems to be clearly inspired by.

That is why he so strongly attacks individualism and undiscipline. Because he wants men in series, individuals as puppets.

According to Taglia, individualism drives the isolated man "to bewitchment, to the search for the quiet little corner where he can neatly arrange his intimate rags, to selfish arrangements, as even an initial spirit of struggle either explodes in a sudden gesture or is exhausted in forms of distrust that are the direct reflection of one's own impotence."

But even when the individual rebels alone, "when he makes the beautiful gesture, there are no social consequences." And his act expresses "a whole social situation already swollen in advance and, for this very reason, falls within the social concreteness of mass struggle."

To such affirmations of the aspiring fascist corporal, it is possible to respond, first of all, that in determining the revolt of the individual, the particular sensitivity of the individual and the irreducibility of his nature influence more than the social situation. So while, in the same situation, others adapt or react with less dangerous means, he explodes in a heroically violent form.

Secondly, it is not true that the act of the isolated individual leaves no social consequences. When the anarchists, acting alone or in a free and revocable agreement with a few companions, called themselves Henry, Ravachol, Caserio, Bresci, Bonnot, Novatore, Pollastro, Di Giovanni, they upset the established society, disrupted its functioning, sparked the spirits, brought the breath of revolt and the strength of disintegration into the herd, and, hated or loved, cursed or admired, imposed themselves on the public's attention and influenced it.

Today, since the anarchists have fallen from the heights of individualism, heroic and illegalist, into the gray swamp of partisan organization, today that they have become respectable people and march unswervingly in the ranks of normality and legality, no one pays attention to them, the masses ignore them, they have no influence on them, and the small party disappears alongside the big ones it imitates. Here, then, is the admirable progress made by the new anarchists.

But Taglia, not limiting himself to deploring only the great rebels and the sterility of their actions, also lashes out against "the atomization of wills," against every form of indiscipline, against "the

ENZO MARTUCCI

Neapolitan vagabond type, *stornellatore*,[41] who lives day to day or ends his individualism, more impatient with logic and coherence than with discipline, in the police barracks."

For Taglia, who dreams of the Spartan life and disciplined soldiers, even "small indiscipline—the chaos of those who cross the street when the light is red, of those who join the army with the intention of hiding, of those who dilute their revolt in the small acts of daily rebellion, of small indiscipline, of small individualism"—is a serious evil.

Instead, I believe that even these mild revolts and minimal indiscipline are not to be condemned but encouraged. Because they represent the beginning of the awakening of the nature suffocated and compressed by coercion and education. They constitute a tendency of the individual to do as they please and not as others want them to, an indifference to the law that obliges them to act as everyone else acts. They reveal a reaction of the personality, free and original, to the absorption into the gregarious mass, a desire to remain oneself and to move in one's own way and not according to the rule. They are, in a word, the first symptom of individual resurgence. They are, potentially, a centrifugal force that, developed into action, would lead to the dissolution of every social organization and every form of regimented life. And if the fascist corporals, who aspire to the perfect barracks, deplore these irrational manifestations and strive to induce man to mark a better pace, I, on the other

---

41   A singer of a type of folk-song called *storntello*. (Ed.)

hand, look upon them with sympathy and enjoy the terror they inspire in all the sacristans of the different churches that prosper in our time.

And for the sacristans, I find only Cambronne's word appropriate.

The writer Mario Mariani sent me a lively polemical letter, to which I responded,

Dear Mariani,

From your letter, I gather that despite claiming to have learned from St. Ambrose that a person can only be offended by themselves, you are actually offended because I pointed out some of the contradictions in your thinking. Punished by resentment, you retorted that I adhere to the here and now and should learn to recognize my own contradictions instead of throwing yours back in your face. However, you added that "the contradiction is not in me or in you but is implicit in the argument and inseparable from it.

You're absolutely right, Mariani! However, you forgot to explain that when someone accepts an argument in which the contradiction is implicit, they must interpret it in one way or another but cannot simultaneously develop it in both opposite directions in which it can be resolved, at least if they want to remain within the realm of logic. Therefore, if the argument is, as in our case, the antinomy between the individual and society, it can be equally demonstrated either that this antinomy is irreducible or that it is resolvable. However, the first solution entails eternal struggle between the individual and society; the second admits final pacification through the sacrifice of the individual to the organized mass. Now, you—an enemy of the state, law, and authority in the name of individual freedom—claim to be able to preserve this integral freedom in your future socialist society, in which only a small number of obligations and sanctions, strictly necessary for the common interest, would be imposed on the individual by the majority. But, dear Mariani, this means wanting there to be a day when there is night, whereas, according to logic, if there is night, there is no day, and if there is day, there is no night. In other words, if there is individual freedom, there are no obligations or sanctions, and if there are obligations and sanctions, there is no individual freedom.

In fact, for the latter, obligations and sanctions, even if they are few and only include "not killing and not stealing," can be felt as a suffocating coercion as terrible as the draconian laws of a despot. And this impediment to the expansion of their life, to their particular way of feeling, is equally painful for the individual, whether it is imposed by the Sun King, the Council of Ten, Masaniello, or a million democratically organized companions. (Democracy is the fashionable lie.)

Secondly, every society tends, by an impulse dictated by the spirit of conservation, to establish within itself the most absolute monism and conformity. Palante has excellently demonstrated this.

Therefore, a society, even if invested with the right to impose on the individual only a few obligations and sanctions, constantly seeks to annihilate the number of these and to first stifle the most serious transgressions of the social pact and then, once the important violations have disappeared, to suffocate, with the same violence, the slight and mild violations. And this continues until the disappearance of even the slightest violation, that is, until the absolute identification, in feeling, thought, and action, of the individual with the organized mass.

Durkheim—a non-individualistic philosopher and sociologist—has argued that the most serious rebellions of the individual against society prevent too tyrannical action exercised by the latter on the individual. Today, in fact, since society has not managed to extinguish the fiercest attacks on the social pact, those attacks that threaten to dissolve it, such as murder and theft, it establishes severe penalties for such crimes and mild penalties for those minor offenses that, such as indecent exposure or nighttime disturbance, do not constitute an attack on the existence of the social pact but still represent a violation of certain of its articles. However, if society were to completely eliminate murder and theft, it would apply the same severe penalties that it currently sanctions for these crimes to indecent exposure and nighttime disturbance because after achieving a first and more important victory over the individual, bending him to the observance of what is fundamental and essential in the pact, it would want to fully bend the

ENZO MARTUCCI

individual, even in less important matters, to absorb him more and more, to identify him with itself. Therefore, in the absence of serious crimes, it would consider the crimes now considered minor as capital offenses and punish them with the utmost severity.[42]

Therefore, dear Mariani, in your socialist society without a state (which, by the way, is quite similar to that of your adversary, the libertarian communists), you would start by sanctioning death against murderers or thieves, and after 50 years, if successful, you would end up applying it against someone who urinates on the street. If in such a society there were no state, this would only happen because the individual would be perfectly assimilated and absorbed by the conformist mass that would replace the state, and we would fall from the frying pan into the fire....

I, on the other hand, consider the antinomy between the individual and society as irreducible. I believe that man, once free again, will be able to associate, if he wishes, with his fellow men and collaborate with them based on a contract that will also contain renunciations of some of his freedoms. But at the moment I want to dissolve the contract, at the moment when I no longer want to recognize it, no one can prevent me from doing so. Society may expel me from its

---

42   In Scandinavian countries, where education prevails and murder and theft are very rare, acts such as harassing a woman or leaving garbage on the street are punished with the utmost severity, whereas such crimes are lightly punished in Latin countries, where, on the contrary, crimes of violence and against property are very frequent.

midst, fight me if I fight it, but it cannot force me to observe a pact that I no longer recognize and cannot pronounce a moral condemnation against me just because I want to regain my full freedom.

In this case, perfect selfishness, free from every bond, can be reconciled with association and the communization of the means of production. I will join the group if I like; I will also stay in it if it suits me; I will leave the group and go against it when I want to. The majority cannot hold me back or force me to follow its way of life. But those who remain united—because they want to—will have the ability to practice any communist, mutualist, cooperative, or other kind of system.

The struggle will remain, it is true. But the struggle is inseparable from life. However, it will become a free struggle, and, precisely because of that, it will lead to balance. When everyone loses the illusion of being protected by social organization, they will prepare their own defense, develop their strength, learn to use every means at their disposal, toughen themselves up, and sharpen their skills. Thus, they will contain the attack of the adversary with their resistance. And if they fall, they will fall with beauty. But when the foolish sheep remains a fool, relying on the cop and the society that are behind him, he is not only fooled by the aggressor but also by society and the cop, who, under the pretext of defending him, enslave him.

The salvation of the individual is in the individual himself. If he can become "unique" with Stirner, "superman" with Nietzsche, "antichrist" with me, if he can regain the freedom of the beginnings and use intelligence and will not to stifle, as he has done so far, natural tendencies but to develop them further, then he will redeem himself.

Otherwise, he will end up as he deserves: under the atomic bomb. And that will be a good thing.

DECEMBER 1948–NOVEMBER 1949.

ALSO AVAILABLE:

The Red Sect by Enzo Martucci
152 pages, 4.25"x6.875", ISBN 978-1-943687-10-7

The Gospel of Power: Egoist Essays by Dora Marsden
390 pages, 6x9", ISBN 978-1944651206

Hyde Park Orator, Illustrated by Bonar Thompson
356 pages, 6x9", ISBN 978-1944651183

*The Radical Book Shop of Chicago: In Which a Disaffected Preacher,
His Blind Anarchist Wife, and Their Precocious Daughters Create an
Important Hub of Literary, Bohemian, and Revolutionary Culture in
Progressive-Era Chicago* by Kevin I. Slaughter
130 pages, 6x9", ISBN 978-1943687282

Might is Right: The Authoritative Edition by Ragnar Redbeard
408 pages, 6x9", ISBN 978-1943687251

A Secret Hit: 150 years of Max Stirner's Der Einzige und sein Eigentum
by Bernd A. Laska
52 pages, 5.5"x8.5", ISBN 978-1-943687-30-5